Chapman

101
Things Every
Boater
Needs to Know

Chapman

101
Things Every
Boater
Needs to Know

Pat Piper

HEARST BOOKS
A division of Sterling Publishing Co., Inc.

New York / London
www.sterlingpublishing.com

Book design by Alexandra Maldonado
Cover design by Margaret Rubiano

Please see page 160 for illustration and photography credits.

Library of Congress Cataloging-in-Publication Data

Piper, Pat, 1953-
  Chapman 101 things every boater must know / Pat Piper.
    p. cm.
  Includes index.
  ISBN 978-1-58816-658-6
  1. Boats and boating—Handbooks, manuals, etc. 2. Seamanship—Handbooks, manuals, etc. 3. Boats and boating—Safety measures. I. Title.
  GV775.P53 2008
  797.1—dc22
                                        2008007844

10 9 8 7 6 5 4 3 2 1

Published by Hearst Books
A Division of Sterling Publishing Co., Inc.
387 Park Avenue South, New York, N.Y. 10016

CHAPMAN and CHAPMAN PILOTING and Hearst Books are trademarks of Hearst Communications, Inc.

Distributed in Canada by Sterling Publishing
c/o Canadian Manda Group, 165 Dufferin Street
Toronto, Ontario, Canada M6K 3H6

Distributed in Australia by Capricorn Link (Australia) Pty. Ltd.
P.O. Box 704, Windsor, NSW 2756 Australia

For information about custom editions, special sales, premium and corporate, please contact Sterling Special Sales Department at 800-805-5489 or specialsales@sterlingpublishing.com.

Manufactured in China

Sterling ISBN 978-1-58816-658-6

Contents

Part 5: The Engine

Part 6: The Electrical System

Part 7: Electronics

Part 10: Bad Weather

Introduction

It's your boat and despite everyone calling you "captain," the fact is, regardless of the title, you *really* are in charge of everyone's well being.

And this means being proactive. Don't wait for things to happen: you need to anticipate events and situations whether it's a possible course change of another boater or the safest way to cross a large wake from a passing boat. Use common sense, avoid unnecessary risks, and always have a Plan B if something goes wrong.

Chapman's 101 Things Every Boater Needs to Know is all about Plan B. These are time-tested solutions to some of the common problems all of us encounter or will encounter on our boats. The difference between "a captain" and "a good captain" is simple: one is a title and the other is a person who gains skill and knowledge every time they go out on the water. The following pages are the result of the experiences of good captains—important lessons that became "Plan B."

Hopefully, some of these strategies may get you and your crew out of a bad situation on the water or—even better—may prevent you from ever getting into such circumstances. If nothing else, the pages that follow will make you a better boater, something all of us can appreciate. Should you want to learn more about being a "good captain," many of the topics covered here are found in greater detail in *Chapman Piloting & Seamanship*.

Pat Piper

1 Boating Basics

Before you cast off a dock line, let's get down to some basics.

	Have a float plan, and let someone on
1	shore know about it

A float plan is a safety measure; it could also be a lifesaver. It's a record of your intended route and the time you expect to arrive back at the dock or boat ramp. Be sure to leave a copy with a friend on shore who has agreed to help out by contacting the marine police or Coast Guard should you fail to return on schedule. Don't call the Coast Guard with your float plan—they won't accept it. The float plan should contain:

- The boat's name, color, make, and model.

- The intended destination with phone number, if available.

- The estimated time of arrival ETA, and the route.

- If layovers are planned, list each one, with phone numbers.

- The number of passengers on board.

- Your cell phone number.

- Coast Guard and marine police phone numbers.

2 Briefing the crew—before they arrive

- Provide the members of your crew—in advance of your departure—with a copy of your float plan. This is not only a courtesy, it will help them determine what to bring with them in terms of food, clothing, fishing equipment, and personal accessories, including medications, if necessary.

- Ask if any has a medical condition, e.g., diabetes, asthma, etc., of which you should be aware. And be prepared to respond, should it become necessary.

- Stress the importance of punctuality. Tides are likely to be an issue in estimating the times of departure and arrival. Emphasize that the success of the trip depends on everyone arriving in time to "make the tide."

- Know what the weather conditions are going to be so you can tell the crew what to expect. If there's a small craft advisory, or if storms are forecast for your area, don't leave the dock.

3 Briefing the crew—when they arrive

- First thing: Show everyone where the life jackets (personal flotation devices [PFD]) are located and how they are put on. If someone chooses not to wear one, ask that at least it always be kept within arm's reach. Should there be any nonswimmers aboard, insist they wear a PFD—at all times—for their own and everyone else's safety.

- Show everyone where the garbage containers are kept. No garbage goes overboard, not even cigarette butts.

- Assign tasks: Make sure each able member of your party is assigned a task related to the smooth and safe operation of the boat—and knows how to do it; for example, instruct

Extra: DON'T OVERLOAD THE BOAT!

Overloading is a major cause of boating accidents. Be sure to check your craft's Capacity Plate, which is required by the U.S. Coast Guard federal Boat Safety Act of 1971. It is required for boats less than 20 feet in length and manufactured after November 1, 1972. Sailboats, canoes, kayaks, inflatable boats, and jet skis are exempt.

The Capacity Plate is usually found on the transom or near the helm. It identifies the maximum weight of persons, engine, and equipment as well as the maximum allowable horsepower of the engine. If you exceed these limits, you stand the chance of voiding your marine insurance policy. If your boat exceeds 26 feet in length, here's a general formula to determine the number of people that can be safely brought aboard (your owners' manual will also have this information):

$$\frac{\text{Boat length (in feet) X Beam (in feet)}}{15}$$

your crew on when and how to place a dock line atop a piling—not in the water; how to fend off; how you intend to leave and in what direction, and what needs to be done as you do. Do the same when returning to the dock/boat ramp/marina, and instruct someone in how to use the boat hook for picking up dock lines.

- Find seating accommodations for those not involved in operational activities.

4   The tool kit

Marine supply stores sell complete tool kits. Make sure yours includes the following and, since they're going to be stored on the boat, that as many of these items as possible are made of stainless steel (stainless steel won't corrode or rust).

- screwdrivers: flat edge and Phillips
- wrenches: adjustable, Allen, and a socket wrench that will fit a spark plug
- a pair of vise grips
- pliers: slip joint and needle nose
- hammer
- hose clamps, stainless steel
- tape: duct and electrical
- a piece of hose large enough to fit over a water/engine hose to repair a leak

- extra: fuel filter, water separator, fuses, screws, washers, bolts, cotter pins
- marine sealant
- replacements bulbs for navigation lights
- replacement batteries for flashlights, handheld GPS and other electronic aids
- combination knife and marlinspike

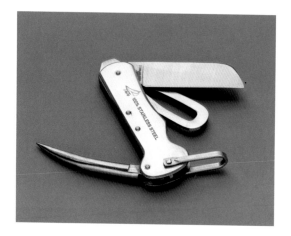

- WD 40
- wire brush
- toothpicks—use them to pry off O rings or lift out impellers from fuel pumps
- voltmeter or digital multimeter

5 The first-aid kit

A first-aid kit should be on board every craft except the very smallest. The extent of its contents will be governed by the distance—actually measured in time—that your boating activities take you from shoreside medical assistance. A number of companies offer first-aid kits designed for various boating needs, ranging from basic kits for day outings and short local cruises to more extensive offshore cruising kits. Here's a basic list of items you will want to consider having at hand.

- adhesive strips, assorted
- adhesive tape, 1-2 rolls
- gauze bandages, 2-inch and 4-inch
- non-stick pads, square, various sizes
- triangular bandages
- butterfly closures
- eye patch
- elastic bandages, various widths
- antiseptic wipes
- antibiotic ointment
- first-aid/burn cream
- lip balm or zinc oxide
- sunscreen
- meat tenderizer or sting relief wipes
- motion sickness tablets
- ammonia inhalants

- aspirin or non-aspirin tablets
- antihistamine tablets non-drowsy formula only
- cold relieft tablets non-drowsy formula only
- oil of clove or toothache remedy
- antacid
- diarrhea medicine
- ice packs
- finger splint
- wire splint
- tweezers
- scissors
- thermometer
- latex or rubber gloves
- hook remover
- sling
- first aid manual
- rescue blanket
- any special medication required by you or a crewmember for individual medical conditions

6   Waypoints and channel markers

If you are heading for a specific destination, make a note of the waypoints and channel markers that will be passed along the course.

7   Trailer boats

If you have a trailer boat, make sure the plug is in before
backing the boat down the launch ramp. According to
BoatU.S. Marine Insurance, missing drain plugs account for
12 percent of all boat sinkings.

Extra: USING A TRAILER?

- Know the weight of your boat fully loaded. The owner's
  manual will give you the "dry weight," which is the weight
  of the hull only. The manual may or may not include the
  weight of the engine. It obviously cannot include the weight
  of all the equipment and personal belongings on board, nor
  the weight of the fuel. (Gasoline weighs about six pounds
  per gallon, ethanol about six and a half.) Water weighs more
  than fuel—a little more than eight pounds per gallon. So be
  sure you know how much fuel and water are onboard.

- Know the tongue weight, i.e., the weight of the trailer
  tongue where it attaches to your tow vehicle. Proper tongue
  weight should be 7 to 10 percent of the combined weight
  of the boat and trailer. If your trailer sways back and forth
  at speeds above 35 mph, low tongue weight is the reason.

---

8   The bilge

Check the bilge. If there is water in it, drain it now and
spend a moment looking into why the water is there.

(The cause is usually rain, especially if the boat has been in a slip in a marina or on a mooring.) If you smell gas, take the time to learn how it got there—a leaking fuel line to the engine? Don't start the engine; fix the problem first, because there are cases of mopping up spilled fuel, starting the engine, and the boat exploding.

9   Fuel supply

Have a general idea how much fuel your engine uses; this way you'll be able to estimate with some accuracy the distance the boat can travel before it becomes necessary to tap a spare fuel tank or look for a fuel stop. And have a few fuel stops in mind; you may not have time to search out a marina with a gas dock.

Extra: ESTIMATING FUEL CONSUMPTION

Fill the tank, go out for a specified period of time, and run the engine at the same speed you'd run it for the trip you're planning to take. Return to the dock and refill the tank, taking note of the amount of fuel that was used. This will help you plan for any extended trips on the water. When estimating your fuel consumption, always use the "one-third" rule: one-third of a tankful to get to your destination; one-third to get back; one-third kept in reserve.

10 The vessel safety check

The marine police, the Coast Guard, or the Coast Guard Auxiliary may stop you on the water to perform a routine vessel safety check to make sure your boat is properly outfitted and sufficiently seaworthy to be underway. This is to ensure your comfort and safety, so—to make sure your trip proceeds without interruption—have the following items on board (you can view the list at www.uscgboating.org/safety/vsc.htm) in plain sight and ready for inspection:

- A personal flotation device (PFD) for everyone onboard.

- A throwable device (seat cushion, horseshoe buoy) if the boat is more than 16 feet long.

- A sound-producing device: a horn capable of a four-second blast that can be heard for a least a half a mile. Attaching a whistle to each PFD, while not required, is nonetheless a good idea.

- Flares that can be used as distress signals.
  (Note: *Always check the expiration date on this equipment and replace as necessary.*)

- At least one fire extinguisher in plain sight.

- Proper ventilation for gasoline engines.

- A backfire flame control for boats built after 1940, powered by gasoline but not an outboard.

- Proper navigation lights.

- If your boat is longer than 26 feet, you'll need a Marine Pollution (MARPOL) placard. This placard lists restrictions on garbage that can't be tossed into the water.

- An operable marine sanitation device if the boat has onboard sanitation facilities.

- Registration numbers properly displayed on the hull and current registration paperwork on board. Have a driver's license for identification.

- If your boat is longer than 39.4 feet, you'll need to have a copy of the Navigation Rules on board.

MARPOL Garbage Dumping Restrictions

Under U.S. federal law, it is illegal to discharge plastic or garbage mixed with plastic into any waters. Regional, state or local regulations may also apply. All discharge of garbage is prohibited in the Great Lakes and their connecting or tributary waters.

Violators are subject to a civil penalty of up to $25,000, a fine of up to $500,000, and 6 years imprisonment.

Open Ocean Restrictions

| Navigable waters & within 3 nautical miles offshore | 3-12 nautical miles offshore | 12-25 nautical miles offshore |

Illegal to dump all garbage!

Illegal to dump garbage > 1"

Illegal to dump floatable packaging, dunnage & lining materials.

Illegal to dump plastics anywhere.

 Report marine pollution incidents to the National Response Center at 1-800-424-8802 or to your local Coast Guard office by phone or VHF radio, channel 16.

Keep our nation's waterways clean-it's the law!

11   Pets on board

Your household pets are part of the family, to be sure. And
the impulse to take them with you, to share in the pleasure of
an outing on the water, is understandable—but give it serious
thought. A pet can require as much attention as a human
passenger, and like humans, are prone to seasickness. Then
there's the question as to how they will be received by your
hosts at docks along your route. Fair weather or foul, be
prepared to take your dog for a walk on the shore from
time to time.

   If you've never taken a pet to sea before, bring him to the
boat in advance of the trip. Let him sit in the boat and get
used to the motion and the surroundings. Don't fire up the
engine until your pet has had a chance to settle in.

12   Boating under the influence (BUI)

According to U.S. Coast Guard statistics, more than
50 percent of all boating accidents and fatalities are related to
alcohol abuse. Alcohol use in a marine environment has
proven to have more of an effect on the human body than the
same amount consumed on land. Because of this, operating
your boat with a cold one in your hand is never a good idea.

Boating under the influence of alcohol—or any other
drug—violates federal law. Don't do it.

2 Underway

The boat is seaworthy; the crew has been briefed; the skipper is prepared. Now what?

Take note of wind, current, and tide as well as any other boats that are nearby because each of these factors plays a role in how you choose to cast off and dock. Talk to each person about the tasks you've assigned him or her: handling lines, fenders, using the boat hook to make a safe departure, and when appropriate, a safe return. If your boat is less than 25 feet long, factor in how each person's weight on the sides affects the stability of the hull.

13 Prop walk

Most single engine outboards have right-handed props, which means, looking toward the bow from the aft of the boat, the propeller turns clockwise. When the propeller is in reverse, the boat will "walk" to port. This can have an effect on departing from as well as returning to the dock or boat slip. Be aware of how your boat responds. If you use twin engines, this isn't as much of an issue.

14 Dock lines in a slip

Once a dock line has been removed from the boat and placed on a piling or the dock, it should remain there. Returning to the slip or the dock with a line in the water is an invitation to getting it tangled in the propeller. Keep the dock lines and spring lines out of the water. And make sure all the dock lines have been released when leaving a dock.

15   Problems leaving the dock

If the wind is against the dock

The key here isn't where the wind is coming from as much as it is the amount of room you have to maneuver in. Cast off all dock lines except for a spring line set amidships and secured toward the stern of the boat on the dock or pier. With the engine in gear (forward) and helm turned toward the dock, gently move the boat so the stern begins to move toward the wind. You may need a fender secured at the bow. Once the stern is pointed toward the wind, release the spring line (someone on the dock will do this) and put the engine in reverse so you can back away from the dock.

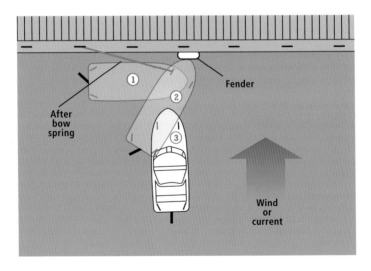

Fender

After bow spring

Wind or current

In tight quarters in a slip

Backing out of a slip or dock with a strong breeze on the bow can be dangerous in a busy harbor or at a gas dock. But this is a common maneuver (you'll need assistance from someone on shore). First, have a forward quarter spring line tied from the dockside rear cleat to a cleat located on the dock amidships. ① Begin backing the boat (the wind may do this without the engine in gear, so go slow) with the helm turned toward the dock. ② You may need a crewmember with a secured fender as the boat begins to pivot on the corner of the dock. ③ The engine should be in reverse at this point. The forward quarter spring line will now pull the boat closer to the dock. ④ At this point it can be released, if there is no traffic, and the engine put into gear.

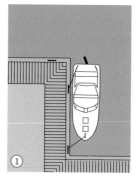

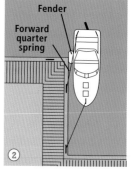

Fender

Forward quarter spring

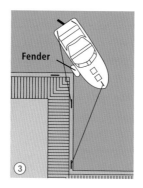

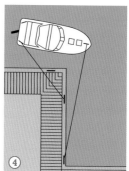

Fender

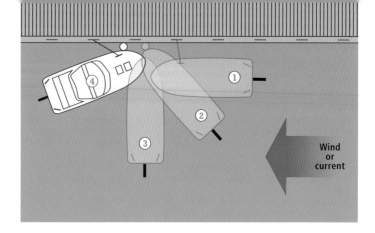

Turning a boat at the dock

It may become necessary, because of wind or currents and close quarters, to turn a boat at the dock for an easier departure. It's easy and can be accomplished without power. If the wind is coming off the stern, let go all lines except for an after bow spring line. Pull the line that forces the stern out into the wind and current. You may need to have a fender positioned on the bow as the boat turns. Transfer the after bowline from one side to the other. If there is no wind or current, you can use the power of the engine to assist with the turning. With an after bow spring line in place, put the engine in gear with a hard right rudder (the helm is all the way over to starboard) if the starboard side is against the dock. If the port side is against the dock, use a hard left rudder.

A fender may be needed to cushion the bow, at which point bring the helm amidships. Ease the spring line and re-rig a second line on the opposite of the bow and toss to shore. With a hard right rudder again, the stern will swing all the way around.

Before you even turn on the ignition, you should have a general understanding of the Navigation Rules, International and Inland. Take a boating course because that's where these rules will be explained and discussed www.uscgboating.org/safety/courses.htm.

The first rule is the most important: Assume the other guy in a boat heading toward you doesn't know the rules. Remember: There is no right of way in a collision. The rules are based on meeting, crossing, and overtaking situations. Here are the basic rules with which you should be familiar.

- When two boats are meeting each other, sound one short blast, alter course to starboard, and pass on the port side.

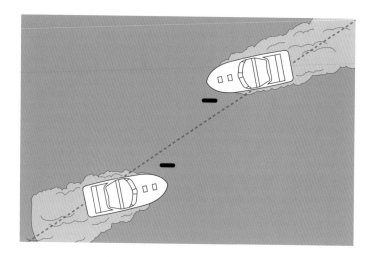

- When two power-driven vessels are crossing each other, the vessel that has the other on its starboard side is the give-way (burdened, colored dark blue) vessel and must take action to avoid collision. It can slow down, stop, or turn to starboard but never to port!

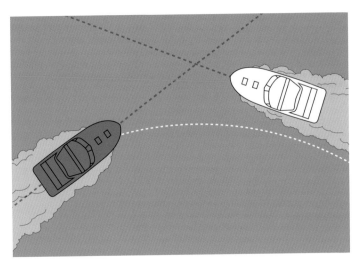

The stand-on (privileged) vessel has the right-of-way and maintains course and speed unless the other vessel fails to take appropriate action.

- When overtaking a vessel, the faster vessel (the one that is overtaking the other) is the burdened vessel and must give way to the boat being passed. If a sailboat is passing a powerboat, the sailboat is the burdened vessel (and gives right of way). The overtaking vessel must keep out of the

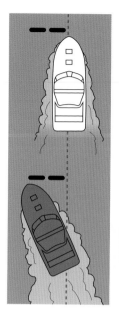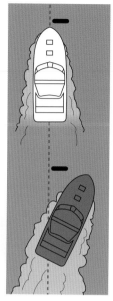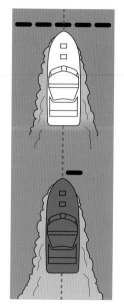

way of the overtaken boat. In some instances (usually on rivers with narrow channels) the overtaking vessel will signal with a horn:

Two blasts: I intend to pass on your port side (left).
One blast: I intend to pass on your starboard side, legal but not recommended (center).
If the action is safe, the vessel being overtaken will respond with similar blasts. If it is deemed unsafe (oncoming traffic, obstruction in the water, anchored boat, or swimmers), the overtaken boat responds with five short blasts indicating that the decision to overtake is unsafe (right).

Extra: SAILBOAT RIGHT-OF-WAY

Think of the word "POW" for sailboat right-of-way. When two sailboats are crossing each other, the PORT boat is the burdened vessel. When one sailboat is passing another in the same direction, the OVERTAKING boat is the burdened boat the same as with powerboats. When two sailboats are going in the same direction, the WINDWARD boat is the burdened vessel.

- In a "no-wake" zone, you must make enough forward speed to maintain headway. Many channels will become "no wake" when marinas are on one or both sides or when the channel narrows. Many lakes have zones that prohibit boats from operating at high speeds within 300 feet of the shore (the permissible distance varies, so check if these rules apply where you will be boating).

- Sailboats have the right-of-way so long as they are under sail and the engine isn't on. Sailing with the engine running—whether in gear or not in gear—is considered the same as being a powerboat. If two sailboats under sail are in a crossing or meeting situation, the vessel on starboard tack (the wind is coming over its starboard side) has the right-of-way.

- Red right return. When entering a harbor or a channel, inbound traffic keeps red channel markers to starboard; outbound traffic keeps green channel markers to starboard.

- Trolling several rods behind your boat doesn't give you right-of-way over other boats. While other boats should understand that you have lines out, it is naïve to believe they will respect your situation. That said, if you see a group of boats fishing in a certain area or trolling together, common courtesy, not right-of-way, tells you to give them space.

- Commercial boats (freighters, tugs with or without barges, cruise ships, ferries) never have the maneuverability of recreational boats. They require longer times to stop; they are limited by depth, and often they can't see your boat at close distances. Stay out of their way.

Extra: TOWING A DINGHY?

If towing a dinghy, utilizing two "painters" (tow lines) will keep it from moving side to side while underway. This can be a single line passed through the bow eye on the dinghy and brought back and secured on the opposite side stern cleat. Tow it no more than 10 to 15 feet behind the boat when underway. When you are coming into a dock or an anchorage, have a crewmember bring the dinghy alongside so it doesn't hit the dock, other boats, or get its line tangled in the prop should you need to use reverse.

When preparing to leave your boat and go to the dinghy dock or cruise around the harbor, always start the outboard on the dinghy before casting off from the boat to make certain it runs. Have a flashlight shining on board when coming back to the boat in the dinghy at night. This will let other boats see you, and it will help you find your boat.

When sailing with a genoa jib that is obstructing the view from the helm, it is necessary to assign a lookout to watch for traffic. At the same time, the helmsman should peek around the sail to keep an eye out for boats. Just because you are on starboard tack, doesn't mean you can sail without keeping watch.

- On a river, the boat coming upriver (against the current) is the burdened vessel and must give way to a boat coming downriver. Boats crossing the current give way to boats coming up or down river.

17 Requesting a bridge to open

When requesting a bridge to open, sound one long blast on your horn followed by one short blast. The bridge tender will respond in the same way if the bridge is to be opened. If it can't be opened right away the bridge tender will sound five blasts. If you have to wait, be aware of the currents because the boat can be pulled into the bridge. You can also contact the bridge tender on VHF Channel 13 or Channel 9 (it varies from area to area). Use 1-watt power. Some can be contacted by cell phone as well.

One more point to be made: If you are approaching an open bridge and the bridge tender signals five short blasts, this means the bridge is going to be closed as soon as the boat currently passing beneath it has done so. Don't try to beat the bridge tender. Acknowledge with five short blasts and stay out of the way.

18 Lights at night

Green lights are on starboard, red on port, and white at the masthead (with a 360-degree view at the top of the boat). If you see white and red, the boat is traveling to port and will cross you.

There may be occasions to use a light to identify unlit navigation marks. Be aware that you can temporarily blind any nearby boaters that are in the line of the light beam.

19 The compass

Despite all the electronics that are available, your compass is the one instrument you must have on board. If the battery on your boat dies or the handheld GPS malfunctions, finding your way back to a familiar mark can be difficult.

You should check your compass at least once a year for accuracy. It's preferable to use a fixed point on land to do this because channel markers and navigation buoys can move over time.

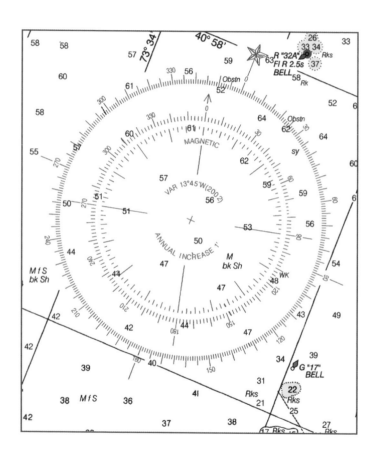

On a chart the inner red compass "rose" shows magnetic north and the outer rose measures true north. The difference is called variation, which changes depending on your location. Navigate using the inner rose. If the readings the compass shows are different than earlier readings, first inspect your pockets. Keys and even a rigging knife can affect the magnetic field around the compass. If you've added speakers or a new dodger or even moved amp meter gauges, all of this can affect compass accuracy. Even the engine block can be the reason for the changes. Consider all these factors before installing a new compass.

Extra: NAUTICAL MILE

One nautical mile equals 5,076 feet. It's also measured as 1 arc minute of latitude. Here's how to make sense of this: If you draw a circle, imagine this is looking down at the earth and the circle is the equator (the poles would, in theory, be the center of the circle). Divide the circle into 360 degrees, similar to what is seen on a compass. Now divide each degree into 60 minutes. The distance between minutes is 1 nautical mile. If you are traveling at 1 nautical mile/hour, you are traveling at 1 knot.

20 Waterskiing, wakeboarding, and knee boarding musts

Being pulled on a water ski or a wakeboard puts you in a world unto itself. But pulling a skier or a boarder requires a few basic steps to ensure that the world behind the boat is a safe one.

- Assign a lookout. The skipper drives the boat; the lookout "looks out" for hand signals and the occasional falls from the skier. If the skier intends to drop a ski in order to slalom, make note of where the ski can be found.

- Agree on a few hand signals.

- Don't take the skier near swimmers, other boats, into shallow water, or near the shoreline.

- Whenever the skier is in the water and near the boat, the engine must be in neutral.

- The skier must wear a PFD.

- Make sure everybody is seated before doing a "hole shot"—pushing the throttle all the way to lift the skier out of the water.

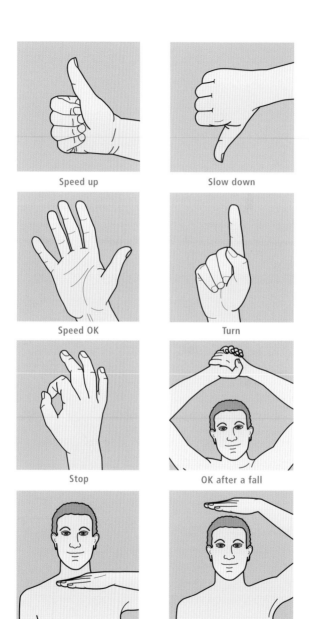

Speed up

Slow down

Speed OK

Turn

Stop

OK after a fall

Cut the motor

Back to the dock

You are going to encounter the waves from the wake of passing boats and you'll encounter the waves from Mother Nature. Both require some thinking ahead by the skipper.

- If you are going to cross wakes or some large waves, alert everyone on board with: "Hang on, here comes a big one!"

- Turn into the wave before it hits. If possible (i.e., if there is no nearby traffic), meet the waves at an angle with the bow of the boat. Don't let the waves hit you sideways, because the boat can be knocked around, possibly injuring passengers. A 45-degree angle will work in most cases. Crossing at a right angle (90 degrees) has the potential of burying the bow as the boat comes down the wave, lifting the prop out of the water and, possibly, the rudder as well.

- Big waves tend to travel in sets, so if you encounter one, you will probably encounter subsequent large waves.

- Slow down when crossing large waves and wakes.

Extra: ESTIMATING DISTANCE

- Distance to the horizon = 1.14 x the square root of your height above the water. Also computed as the square root of your height above the water x .5736.

- If you can see individual windows of a house on shore, you are two miles out. If you see a beach, you are four miles out.

- To convert knots to miles per hour, multiply knots by 1.15.

22 Boating at night

As with an automobile, operating a boat at night is much different from operating one in daylight. While it's important to understand your course when the sun is out, it's all the more important to know your direction and position relative to shore and shallow water when the sun has set.

- Go slow. Even with GPS waypoints and radar, it is going to be easier to correct a mistake (and possibly save the boat) when moving through the water slowly.

- Turn the brilliancy of all electronic screens in the cockpit down so as not to "blind" your view beyond the bow. If using a flashlight on board, cover it with a red sock for the same reason.

- When operating a spotlight, don't blind other boaters by shining it directly at them.

- Be aware fish markers, crab pots and/or lobster traps, and fishing weirs aren't lit at night. Have a lookout assist you through these areas.

- Turn the satellite radio/stereo off. Unlike the situation on a highway, boats can approach from any direction, and the sound of a boat may be heard long before its navigation lights are seen.

Bowline

This is the most useful of all knots on board a boat. Once learned (and practice is necessary), it is easy to make, never slips or jams, and can always be untied. Two bowlines, one on each line, are an excellent combination when you need to tie two lines together.

Bowline

Cleat Hitch—Cleating a Line

Use the line on the cleats normally located on the boat's bow. Sailboats also have cleats near the winch to secure a jib sheet. The cleat design "locks" the line at the first turn.

Start with a turn around the cleat, then go around the cleat so that the line passes under each horn once. Finish with a half hitch over one horn. More wrappings and hitches are not needed, and they only slow the process of casting off.

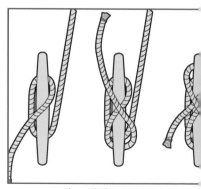

Cleat Hitch

Clove Hitch

The Clove Hitch is used to temporarily tie a boat to a piling. It can be done quickly but one needs to keep an eye on possible slippage. It is made of identical half hitches placed on top of each other around a piling or a spar. A clove hitch always has part of the line "crossing" diagonally over the rest of the knot.

Clove Hitch

Sheet Bend

This is an excellent way to tie two lines together, especially if they are of different sizes or textures. As you will realize when you practice tying knots, some are just variations on a theme. You can use part of a sheet bend to fasten onto a loop.

Sheet Bend

3 Anchoring and Mooring

Being at anchor or on a mooring can be relaxing, but most of the conversation about anchors isn't about problems getting them into the water, it's about getting them out of the water. Moorings can also be a challenge for both crew and skipper. In both instances, things can go wrong, and quick action is needed to prevent a restful experience from becoming a nightmare.

24   The anchor is dragging

Whenever this happens, the skipper has to make a decision if the boat has the potential of hitting other boats or being damaged by nearby rocks or going aground. If so, fire up the engine, have someone on the bow bring the anchor rode in and make another attempt to set the anchor.

If there is no imminent danger, check the amount of scope that has been played out. In many cases, that's all that is required. A common mistake boaters make is not factoring in the distance from the bow of the boat to the water when deciding on scope length. If a 7:1 scope is used (and this is  the common formula—7 feet for every foot of depth), but the height of the anchor line above the water isn't included, this can be the problem, especially if the current or winds are strong. Slowly pay out more scope, occasionally "snugging" (a brief tug on the line to help set the anchor) it to ensure the anchor is beginning to grab the bottom. Your anchor line should be marked every ten feet with depth indicators (usually a plastic tag that is sewn into the line) so you can measure the water's depth.

Extra: SCOPE

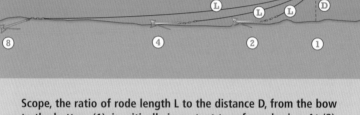

$$Scope = \frac{Length}{Distance}$$

Scope, the ratio of rode length L to the distance D, from the bow to the bottom (1), is critically important to safe anchoring. At (2) the rode length is twice the distance D, but the angle of pull tends to pull the anchor free. At (4), with L four times D, the anchor can dig in, but there is still too much upward pull on the rode. At (8), scope 8:1, the short length of chain at the anchor lies flat on the bottom, and any pull acts to pull the anchor in deeper.

Extra: ANCHOR CHAIN

The anchor will have better holding power if a length of chain is attached to the anchor and then to the line. This helps the anchor set itself into the bottom.

SCOPE HOLDING POWER

The ratios and percentages below indicate the ability of an anchor to hold a boat according to the amount of scope put into the water. For example, with a rode length of 80 feet in 40 feet of water, a 2:1 scope, the holding power of the anchor is only 35% of its potential hold. The point of this chart is to graphically show that the more line put into the water, the greater the holding power of the anchor.

Scope Ratio	Percentage of Potential Holding Power
2:1	35%
3:1	53%
4:1	67%
5:1	77%
6:1	85%
7:1	91%
10:1	100%

25   The anchor is still dragging

Turn on the engine and move the boat forward (into the wind or the current, whichever is stronger), put it in neutral, let the boat fall back while again "snugging" the line to give the anchor more bite. Now put the engine in reverse and gently let the boat try to reset the anchor in the bottom. Put the engine in neutral and take note of your position with a pair of landmarks that are lined up on shore (i.e., a tree close to the shoreline and a tree farther away; a person sitting on the beach and an antenna farther away).

26   The anchor is still dragging—Part 2

It's time to pull up the anchor and try to reset it. If the bottom is rocky, you may need to change the type of anchor being used (a danforth is good in sand and mud but won't work in rocks; a CQR works well in grass; a yachtsman's anchor is preferred when anchoring in rocks). If you can add more chain to the ground tackle, this, too, could keep the anchor rose horizontal to the bottom.

Extra: THE SENTINEL ("KELLET")

If you have only one anchor and the winds are increasing, consider the use of a sentinel as a way to keep the force of the boat going over the waves from making the anchor drag. Also called a "kellet," the sentinel is nothing more than a weight that is attached with a ring to the rode using a second line and sent half the distance to the anchor (small mushroom anchors have been used in the past if a heavy weight can't be found). When in place, the sentinel allows the anchor chain and rode to pull horizontally across the bottom, allowing the anchor to set all the more securely.

Another option is the use of a plastic foam buoy on the surface with one end attached to the anchor rose and the other attached to a line going to the boat. This works well because the boat's bow is being pulled into the waves from the anchor below the surface. The downside is small boats may not have room to carry a buoy.

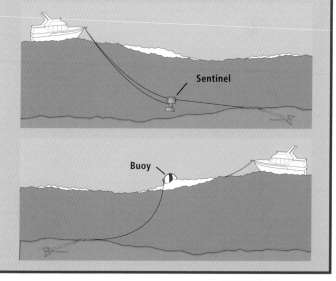

Sentinel

Buoy

27   The anchor is snagged

Boaters report dropping their anchors on jagged rocks that refuse to release the flukes of the anchor, or on old tires where the anchor becomes entangled in the opening of the sidewall, or even on sunken shopping carts and underwater cables. The first attempt at releasing the anchor should be pulling the line from the opposite direction, which, in most cases, entails motoring so that the bow is facing opposite of where it is now.

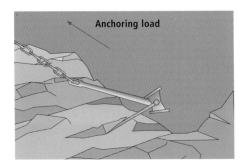

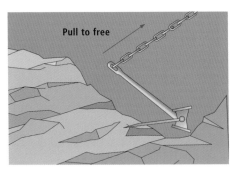

Scowing is a technique that "pulls" the anchor from its crown off the bottom. Attach the anchor rode to the anchor crown and then run it back along the shank to the ring. Lash the anchor ring and the rode (usually a chain) together. Should the anchor become lodged on the bottom, the lashing will break with the force of the pull and the anchor can then be lifted off the bottom from the crown rather than the ring. Twist ties are a commonly used lashing, though some boaters prefer a light lashing of marline. Tying the marline with an overhand knot with an extra turn should hold everything in place until pressure is applied. However, if the winds are shifting or the tides are changing, the boat will swing, possibly pulling the anchor out of the bottom prematurely.

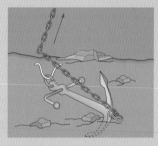

Extra: THE BRIDLE

While a mooring line works fine when hauled aboard and secured on the bow, some boaters prefer to use a bridle so that the boat is centered. Single handers use this method by cleating a line on one side of the bow, running it through a chock, passing the line around the outside of the bow and any stanchions on the side on which you intend to pick up the mooring. Then, with the engine in neutral, position the boat's corner of the stern next to the mooring where you can slip the line through the pennant and walk it back to the bow, where it is passed through a deck chock and secured on the cleat.

28   The anchor is snagged—and it's time to leave

Cut the anchor line, but mark it with a float to keep unknowing boaters from wrapping their props around it. Anchors (and chain and rode) can be replaced.

29   The mooring ball pennant

Can't pick up the mooring ball pennant (the line with a loop that is pulled aboard and secured)? If it's possible, assign one person to grab the mooring pennant with the boat hook, lifting it so that a second person can grab it and pull it under the bow pulpit (if applicable) before tying it off on a cleat or bitt. The helmsman needs to communicate with the person(s) on the bow so that everyone knows hand signals for "put the engine in neutral," "go to port," and "go to starboard." The key to getting a mooring is to approach from downwind going into the wind toward the pennant slowly. The boat should have no forward motion when the mooring ball is at the bow. The second most important thing to know is if you can't make a successful grab on the first pass, make a second pass (and, if necessary, a third and a fourth). Yes, there may be an audience on shore or other boats, but they aren't a part of this maneuver.

Note: Public mooring balls have a horizontal blue stripe. Don't pick up a private mooring unless you have permission to do so.

Extra: THE "MOB" BUTTON

Some boaters will set their position on a GPS by hitting the "mark" or "MOB" button on their GPS and (if applicable) set an alarm to record any errant movement while at anchor.

---

30 Heavy winds while at anchor

Set out two anchors at 45-degree angles to each other. This can be done if there is room to maneuver in the anchorage. Since high winds are expected, try to use 10:1 scope on both anchor rodes. With the bow pointed directly into the wind, the first anchor should be set halfway between the beam and the bow, and then the same angle should be used on the opposite side. The result will be 45 degrees.

31 The three-anchor method

A variation of the two-anchor technique is to use a third anchor, setting it in the direction from which the wind is coming. However, in the event of hurricane preparation, use the "Star Mooring"—three anchors set 120 degrees from one another (the boat is in the center) and all three rodes are secured at the bow. This way it always points into the wind during shifts.

32 The anchorage is crowded

If you are anchoring near other boats, remember they don't have to move lines or change positions to accommodate you. The burden is on you to find a suitable spot where your boat is not going to interfere with everyone else (crossing anchor lines and hitting boats when swinging during wind shifts are two considerations). This might be the time to try a two-anchor Bahamian mooring, which is putting one anchor off the bow and a second off the stern with both rodes (each with the same scope) secured on the bow. The boat won't swing as much as it would if it were on a single anchor.

Extra: DON'T ANCHOR FROM THE STERN

Unless you are fishing for a brief period of time and unless the water is calm and unless you are going to be on board the boat, don't anchor from the stern. On many outboard designs, there is a low cutout to accommodate the engine(s), and this is where a passing wake or sudden waves can swamp a boat.

Many boats traveling together for a picnic or an overnighter will choose to raft up. In rafting, only one boat should be anchored. The other boats are made fast to it so that all will move as a unit. Raft only in light breezes and in calm water. When doing a raft up, one boat comes in first and drops its anchor and makes sure it is set. The second boat pulls alongside (with fenders on both sides) and tosses both a bowline and a stern line (stay 6 to 10 feet away from the anchored boat when doing this). The boat is then snugged up against the anchored boat and a third comes alongside. Be sure bow and stern lines go through deck chocks and/or never above lifelines or rails.

4

Aground

Running aground is something you'll realize very quickly—the boat will slow, despite giving it more throttle, until it becomes motionless. Usually it will happen with all your friends aboard—never when you're alone. Either way, it has the potential for becoming a very bad situation. If you're lucky, sometimes the wake from a passing boat can provide just enough extra depth to move the boat. If you're not lucky, here's what to do—and not to do.

34 Don't back up!

Ignore the first reaction to retrace your steps or put the boat in reverse to back out. Instead, do the following:

- Quickly put the engine in neutral. If hard aground, shut the engine off and check for any hull leaks. If any are seen, the first question becomes is it safer to keep the boat aground with a leak than trying to find deeper water where the boat could actually sink?

- Next, if in tidal waters, determine if the tide is rising or falling (a common way of determining tidal change is to look at nearby fishing pots or navigation marks because you can easily see the direction in which the water is moving). If the tide is rising and no leaks are found after inspecting the bilge, stuffing box, and hull, doing nothing more than waiting for enough water to float the boat may be the most sensible action. If the tide is falling, you've got to make some quick decisions.

35   How to determine the depth of the water

Consult your charts and determine where the deeper water is located. If you have a dinghy, now is the time to put it to use with a lead line (this can be made quickly with a weight on one end and dropped into the water to measure depth) or even an extended boat hook and take soundings (check water depths) near the boat. Get a sense of where the closest and, if rocks are involved, safest deeper water is located.

36   Powerboat tactics

If you have an outboard engine or an I/O, start it up and then tilt it up so that the prop remains in the water and try slowly backing out—move the crew to the stern as well. But if there is any indication of sand or silt being kicked up, turn the engine off. Sand or silt can clog the water-intake strainer or water-pump impeller of the engine, which can cause the engine to overheat. If the stern is on the bottom, there is also a chance of damaging the rudder by trying to use reverse to get into deeper water. Be very careful.

- Kedge the anchor. Toss it out, float it out, swim it out to deeper water, let it set, secure it to a cleat and then try to pull the boat with the anchor line. If there is a current or a tide, position the anchor in the direction of the current

---

Extra: THE ANCHOR LINE

Attach an anchor line to the main halyard, take the anchor out into known deeper water with the dinghy, or float it on a boat cushion with the standing end of the line in your hand, letting it drift into deeper water (sometimes it can be pushed toward deeper water with the boat hook), pull the line that is attached to the cushion, letting the anchor drop to the bottom, and allow it to set with occasional tugs. Then winch in the halyard. The boat will lean and may begin to refloat. If necessary, swim the anchor out.

---

or tide. By doing this you may be able to use the wakes of passing boats to pull on the line and move the boat as the waves go under the hull.

37   Sailboat tactics

Gather the crewmembers on one side of the boat with a few leaning out with hands on the shrouds as a way to lean the boat to one side, thus taking the keel off the bottom. Sometimes a few crewmembers can go over the side and help push the boat off if the bottom is soft and they are wearing personal flotation devices.

38   Lightening the boat

Consider draining the water tank (water weighs 8.3 pounds per gallon). Sometimes, coolers are filled with melted ice. If it's possible, put all the extra items in the dinghy.

39   Outgoing tide—and nothing works

You need to determine if the boat is sitting on rocks, stones, sand, silt, or clay. If it is a sailboat, and the bottom is rocky, the boat is going to lean to one side as the water depth decreases, so use both cushions and fenders to brace the boat—and protect the hull—to keep it as upright as possible. This is also a good time to set out a few anchors.

40   Assistance from another boat

By now you should have an anchor out toward deeper water to ensure the boat doesn't drift any shallower than it already has. If an offer of assistance is made from a passing boat, take the following into consideration:

- Is the water deep enough so that a brief tow from the other boat won't damage the hull?

- How will the towline be passed between boats?

The Monkey Fist is used to make a ball at the end of a heaving line. Make three loops around your hand, some 4 feet from the end of the line. Take the working end to make three more loops around, at right angles to the first three. The final set of loops is made around the inner group. Insert a pebble, if needed, and work turns to take up the slack.

- Can the other boat get close enough to get a towline to you without going aground itself?

- Is the deck cleat that will be used for the tow strong enough to handle the force that will be placed on it? This is the moment to see if there is a backing plate on any cleat that is going to be used. Otherwise the force could pull the cleat out of the deck.

- Raise the outboard and the I/O.

- Talk to the skipper of the assisting boat (VHF will help) and agree to slowly pull the towline taut before gently increasing the throttle. Do not gun the engine. Go slow and gently increase speed if the boat begins moving.

41   Assisting a grounded boat

One of the cardinal rules about boating is to provide help when it's needed and only if it doesn't make a potentially bad situation worse. Another rule is that there are three kinds of boaters: those who have run aground; those who haven't done it yet; and those who are liars. Offering assistance is the right thing to do, but consider these issues when seeing a boat in shallow water:

- Can you get close enough without putting your boat and crew in danger? What is the draft of your boat and what is the depth of the water near the boat that is aground?

- If the boat needing assistance is still floating, a wake from your boat may be all that is needed. Just be sure the boat needing assistance has an anchor out for kedging.

- Can you offer a towline (or take a towline) bow first and then back out without interference from the tide, current, or wind? If you back in, how close can you maneuver without putting your boat in peril? If the line is to be thrown, consider doing it with a Monkey Fist knot (page 67) to make the toss easier. If there isn't time to do the knot and you are close enough to toss a line, always throw the line above the person who is going to catch it. This way it is easily grabbed.

- Stay away from the towline on both boats. If a cleat is torn out of the hull or the line snaps, anyone in the way can be seriously injured. If a boat can't be safely towed or ungrounded, call a professional towing service.

- Never try to pull a grounded boat in reverse. Always secure the towline at the stern and slowly proceed forward toward deeper water. Or, depending on wind and current, consider putting the towline amidships and pull at an angle to the wind.

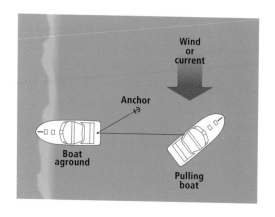

- If the wind or current is broadside to you, both your boat and the grounded boat should have anchors placed upwind and forward. This way, the pulling boat won't be pulled into shallow water when the grounded boat frees itself.

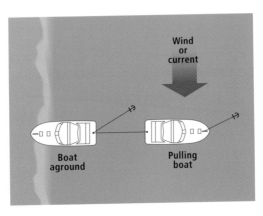

- If the grounded boat—or the pulling boat—doesn't have a secure cleat around which a towline can be attached, there is one more option before calling for professional assistance: Put a line around the hulls secured with cushions or fenders at pressure points and then make a bridle using three bowlines—one at the ends of the line going around each hull and then a towline between the boats with a bowline at each end. This distributes the strain of both boats more evenly and thus results in less chance of damage. Be sure to pad pressure points to guard against chafing or scarring.

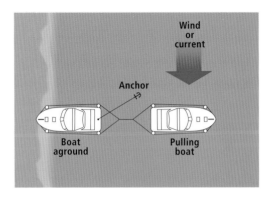

Wind or current

Anchor

Boat aground

Pulling boat

42   Calling for help

If all else fails, this may be the time to call a professional tower for assistance. Many recreational boaters are willing to offer help, and if you accept, make sure there is agreement on what needs to be done.

When you call, know how to direct the towboat to your location. For example, a towboat operator may be told, "I can see the Arial Bridge." But are you north or south of the bridge. Is there a channel marker nearby that you can identify? How many miles offshore are you? Can you provide waypoints on your GPS? Be ready to give a description of your boat, how many are on board, and if there are any medical concerns.

One more point to be made: Use the cell phone sparingly. This is a time when the battery needs to remain powerful to maintain contact with the tow operator. If you need to cancel a restaurant reservation, that is the cordial thing to do, but don't wear down the battery of the phone. Remember, the towboat operator may be trying to reach you because he's having trouble locating your boat. Use VHF whenever possible. If your cell phone battery is wearing out, you can use the marine operator channels on VHF (channels 24, 25, 27, 84, 85, 86, 88) to contact people on shore, but remember, any boater with a receiver will be able to hear your conversation. Keep an eye on your boat's battery charge too. You'll want to be able to start the engine when the boat is in deeper water.

Extra: TOWING OR SALVAGE?

Whenever a commercial towboat renders assistance to a boater, the issue of whether this is towing or salvage comes into question. Being towed off a sandbar or being towed simply because a water pump has failed in the middle of nowhere usually isn't a big deal. But if your boat has hit a rock and is now leaking fuel or drifting into a seawall or is in a situation that presents imminent peril to the environment, life, or navigation, then it is a salvage job, meaning the tower can set a higher price or ask for a portion of the boat's value.

That's why it's so important to ask if this is towing or salvage before the tower begins work. Usually the tower will tell you upfront, but if he doesn't, the burden is on you to ask. Remember, you don't have to sign anything. However, never sign a *Lloyd's Open Form Salvage Contract* or any document that has blanks the tower/salvor says will be filled in later. This can keep you in the courts for years. There are mediation boards for these disputes. If unresolved, matters of salvage go before a Federal Admiralty Court.

5

The Engine

Marine engines have become complex mechanical and electronic systems as much in need of computers as they are of wrenches to maintain and operate. This is why a warranty can be jeopardized if clumsy attempts are made to fix something when the engine fails to operate properly. But despite the hi-tech devices they contain, there are still a few steps that can be taken before calling for assistance from a towboat service or a licensed technician.

Do this first: Make the boat as safe as you can. Get it away from traffic, drop the anchor, keeping in mind the potential for a tidal change (if the boat is hard aground, starting the engine isn't going to matter). Then take a moment to relax and begin with some engine basics, because most of the time this is where the cause of the trouble is to be found.

43 If the engine won't run

First check the throttle control lever at the helm. If it is inadvertently left in gear (forward or reverse), the engine isn't going to run. This is done as a safety precaution to ensure the engine is never started in gear. If the boat is older, jiggle the throttle control back and forth while turning the key. That may be all that is required.

44   Know the "sound" of your engine

Engines need fuel, air, and electricity to run. If one of these elements is missing, the engine is going to let you know, and quickly. After running the engine with all these factors in play, you'll begin to "hear" when something isn't right. Get to know the sound of your engine.

45   Fuel supply

If an engine won't start, first check the fuel. Sometimes a fuel gauge isn't accurate, so think back to when the tank was last filled and how many hours the engine has run since that time. It may be dry. If there is fuel, take a look at the fuel lines for improper connections or kinks and twists that can prevent fuel getting from the tank into the engine.

If you spill fuel at the gas dock, a solution of white vinegar and dishwashing liquid will clean the surface. Many gas docks keep clay kitty litter on hand for this purpose. Don't let the spilled fuel get into the water.

46   Bad fuel

When was the tank last filled and how long has the engine been running since that time? If the fuel in the tank hasn't been used since the most recent fill up, the problem is likely to be water in the fuel. This occurs because of condensation: temperature changes cause water to form in a gas tank, or even a storage tank, before it ever gets to your gas tank.

Because gasoline is lighter than water, it floats above water in the tank. As the fuel is drawn into the system, water gets in, and you'll notice a loss of power or an inability to run under a load. So check the fuel filter/water separator in the engine. Many have a clear bowl on the bottom where any water present can be detected. If this is the case, unscrew the bowl, empty the water, check the filter, and try to start the engine again.

47   Air supply

The vent on the gas tank (usually a portable tank) may be closed. Open it.

48   Electrical system

Check the battery cables to ensure there is a solid connection with no corrosion on the positive and negative posts. Now check the leads to the engine.

- Inspect the fuses. If you have a battery selector switch, move it to the second battery or to "both" and try to start the engine.

- Inspect the spark plugs. The electrode (this is the tip that goes into the engine) should be free of heavy carbon buildup and oil. When replacing, add a small amount of anti-seize compound to the threads of the plug. At the other end, the rubber/plastic covering should be pressed tightly to the top of the plug.

49   When the engine overheats

First take a look to see if water is coming out of the engine: on outboards the water that is pumped through the engine to cool it is located on the shaft just below the engine cover, while on diesels and I/Os it's on the transom at about water level. (*Note:* If no water is coming out of the outboard, poke a needle into the hole first because the line could be clogged with dirt.) Check the water intake for a plastic bag or other debris that may have become wrapped around the opening so that water can't be pulled into the engine.

■ Inspect the seacock to make sure it is open or if sand or mud has been pulled in during a recent grounding or passage through shallow water.

- Zebra mussels and barnacles can block the engine's water intake. If you suspect this to be the cause of the overheating, before hiring a diver to do the job, try the following:

  1. Close the seacock and remove the water intake hose.
  2. Attach a long hose to the seacock, holding it upright and well above the waterline (otherwise, your cabin is going to start flooding).
  3. Open the seacock and push a metal rod or coat hanger through the hose, knocking the intake blockage out of business.
  4. Check the belt on the circulation pump or raw water pump. If broken and no spare is available, boaters have made a temporary "belt" out of 3/8-inch line.

50   When the engine shuts down

If the engine runs in neutral but shuts down under load, the prop may have a line or weeds wrapped around it. Shut down the engine first; then inspect the prop.

Diesel Engines

Diesel engines differ from internal combustion engines in a single way. Unlike the two-stroke or four-stroke outboard, a diesel engine doesn't require spark plugs. Instead, air is heated in the cylinder when it is compressed. Fuel is sprayed into the compressed air and ignites because of the high temperature.

Diesel engines are more expensive but get better mileage than the internal combustion two- and four-stroke engines. Diesels operate at hotter temperatures than their gasoline counterparts and are common on boats designed for long cruises (trawlers and private yachts).

Extra: USING A VOLTMETER ON THE BATTERY

- Your boat's battery produces direct current so you need to set the voltmeter to DCV (12 volts direct current). (The outlets in your home use alternating current, so in that case you'd set the voltmeter to ACV.)

- The red probe of the voltmeter should be attached to the positive post of the battery, while the black probe is attached to the negative post.

- Fully charged, the battery will deliver 12.6 volts. At 75% charge, the battery delivers 12.4 volts, and this isn't enough to turn over the starting motor.

51   If the engine doesn't start

If the starter doesn't turn the engine over, do the following (you'll need a voltmeter).

- Check for 12 volts (DC) at the battery. If fewer than 12 volts, either you need to get a new battery (if allowed to drop voltage for an extended period of time, many lead acid batteries cannot be recharged) or to charge the existing one.

- Check for 12 VDC at the big wire leading to the starting solenoid (normally mounted on the starter motor). If there is enough voltage in the battery but not here, check for dirty contacts or a faulty battery switch.

- Check for 12 VDC at the other side of the solenoid (this is usually a flat copper stock or very thick wire leading to the starter motor) with the starter button pressed. If this step shows no results, the solenoid needs replacing. But you can get around it temporarily with a technique called "jump the key," which involves connecting a wire from the 12 VDC positive (a large terminal on the back of the solenoid that leads to the battery) to the small terminal that has a white wire attached to it on the back of the solenoid. This bypasses the entire ignition switch circuitry. If the engine turns over, then the ignition switch or some internal fuse in the switch circuit or (most likely) cruddy contacts in that circuit are at fault. If this still doesn't produce results, you most likely need a new starter motor.

If the engine turns over rapidly (not ahh-yug, ahhh-yug but zitta-zitta-zitta) and won't start, it is either because of a clogged air filter (unlikely on a boat) or no fuel. Check the primary filter to see if it's full of water or if the filter element is clogged.

52   Diesel exhaust

When a diesel engine starts, it will produce white smoke for about five minutes. If this continues for a longer period of time, there may be deposits around the piston rings, which, if left unattended, can result in more serious problems later on. If you see blue smoke after a while, there's engine oil in the combustion chamber. Black smoke suggests the air cleaner needs to be cleaned or replaced. Or that there is incorrect fuel injection timing or the engine is being overloaded (too much weight on board).

53   Air in the system

Air may also be getting into the system, so you must bleed the engine. First look for fuel leaks in the hose between the lift pump (it pumps fuel from the fuel tank to the engine) and the fuel injection pump. Also check injector pipes for leaks (unlikely). Air may be getting into the system between the fuel tank and the fuel lift pump. Is the primary filter tight?

Did you use zero or two or more gaskets? Only one will work. Leaks between the tanks and the lift pumps mean that air is sneaking in and not that fuel is leaking out, since the lines are under negative pressure.

54   Back pressure

If the engine is turning over, be sure to drain the muffler and/or disconnect the water line between the engine heat exchanger and the muffler, so that cooling water will not fill up the muffler, creating enormous back pressure. Even if the engine won't start, the water pumps will be spinning and doing their job.

Dirty fuel is the most common cause of a rough running engine. Change the fuel filter(s); you may have to do this several times before the engine runs as it should. Try running the engine using a different fuel tank (or if possible, from a portable fuel tank). If after doing this and the engine runs smoothly but the fuel is still dirty, there may be algae in the fuel tank.

If the fuel is bad and you have no replacement fuel filters, pantyhose has been known to work as temporary fix.

Don't worry about the timing slipping, and definitely don't mess with it. It's time to get professional help if you think this is a problem.

Fuel tanks may or may not have shutoffs, but this is also something to check out.

Outboard Engines

55   If the engine won't start

Look at the emergency kill switch lanyard. If it is removed, reattach it to the throttle. In fact carry a spare emergency kill switch lanyard in the event you lose the one now attached to the engine.

56   Choke setting

If the engine hasn't been run, make sure the choke has been opened. If it has been run, begin with the choke closed as if it would be running. If unsuccessful, open the choke halfway and try again.

57   Primer bulb

If the outboard fails to start, have someone squeeze the primer bulb while you try to start the engine. If you smell gas, STOP. There's a leak in the fuel line.

Inboard/Outboard (I/O) Engines

Over time, engine bellows become dry and brittle, so look for evidence of cracks or holes in the folds. If you find any, it's time to replace the bellows. If your boat is in salt water, inspect the bellows more often. Heat is a drying element of bellows.

Muskrats have become an insidious nuisance for boaters. Raise the outdrive and turn it to starboard as a way to keep them from lingering in the bellows. This has become such a problem that some manufacturers now offer an anti-rodent device that can be attached to the outdrive when docked. The shift cable has also become a favorite muskrat target.

58   Oil leaks

Older inboard/outboard engines may lose oil, and the first place to check—if the dipstick reading is low—is the bilge. This is because the oil pan sits in or just above the bilge, and water can corrode the pan to the point that a small leak can begin to drain the oil.

59   Distributor caps

Depending on the design of the I/O, the distributor cap may be located in the lower part of the engine box and toward the transom. Rainwater or even spray from being underway can find its way to the cap and shut down the electrical charge in the engine. Spray WD-40 or CRC-56 (moisture displacement) on the cap and the wires leading to it.

6 The Electrical System

A towboat operator, when asked what was the most common problem he encountered when doing his job, answered with one word: "Batteries." The battery is the center of your boat's electrical system, and when it stops, so does everything else.

60 The battery is dead

While the battery may appear to be dead, take a look at the fuses and circuit breakers (if applicable). Use the process of elimination to find the source of the problem. First, check that the switch is on at whatever unit isn't working (once again, the obvious is often the culprit). Then check the switch panel.

61 The battery is still dead

Examine the battery posts to see if the contact points have become dirty. Remove the negative cable (black) on the battery first, and then remove the positive cable (red). Keep in mind that there may be a pair of black cables on the negative post: one is the negative battery cable and the other is the ground, which is connected to the engine block. DISCONNECT the cables and mix a solution of 1 tablespoon baking soda per 1 cup water and brush it on each battery post. Let it soak for a minute (it will bubble). Clean it off with a paper towel, coat each post with battery terminal grease or corrosion lubricant (Vaseline works well), reconnect the positive cable first and then connect the negative cable.

One can also purchase anticorrosion rings that are placed on both the positive and negative posts to keep contact points clean. A battery-post cleaner works too (it's a wire

Extra: FUSE FACTS

Fuses protect against overload and short circuits. Each is rated by amps for the instrument (VHF, DVD) being protected and the size of the wire (measured as "awg" and labeled as "gauge") to which it is connected (an example would be a 50-amp fuse connected to a 6-gauge or 6 awg wire). As a result there may be fuses of differing ratings used on different circuits, which is why you must carry spares for each circuit.

- Glass fuses tend to suffer from vibration in fuse-holder sockets, and on boats some corrosion also appears when they are exposed to moist salt air. This often leads to bad contacts and intermittent power supply.

- The fuse elements can age over time if running hot and close to maximum, and they may blow even if there is no fault.

- The automotive knife type of fuse tends to be a lot more resilient to vibration and corrosion.

- You should never put larger fuses into a circuit if a smaller rated one is blowing. When a fuse blows it means something is wrong. If you insert a larger rated fuse into a circuit you may end up causing a fire as the circuit overheats.

brush placed over the post and turned to loosen dirt). If it is a wet-cell battery, check the water levels in each cell and fill if necessary, using distilled water only.

62   Wiring problems

Most wiring problems occur at the connections. If the problem is only a specific instrument, trace the wiring from the instrument that isn't working, looking at the connection to the instrument and then the connection to the circuit breaker and/or fuses. No bare wires should be visible.

63   Jumper cables

If a nearby boat has offered you assistance and one of you has jumper cables (and they are long enough), the procedure is no different from that used in jumping a car battery. The engine on the boat with the good battery should be off. Connect the dead battery first and then connect to the good supply battery on the other boat. One jumper cable goes on negative post to negative post and the other cable goes on the positive post of the good battery to the positive post of the bad battery (always connect positive LAST, and once the engine is running, remove LAST).

   Once the engine starts, disconnect the jumper cables (negative FIRST) and determine if the alternator is recharging the battery. If it isn't, you may not be able to restart the engine, so the next step should be back to the dock or boat slip or boat ramp. If one boat hull is metal— don't connect the jumper cable from the negative post to

Extra: CHECKING BATTERY-CHARGE STATUS

To check the battery-charge status of a wet-cell battery (also called "lead acid"), take a multimeter or voltmeter, set the dial to DC (direct current), place the negative lead on the negative terminal and the positive lead on the positive terminal. Each cell should produce about 2.1 volts, so at full charge the battery should show a minimum of 12.6 volts. Don't let the battery discharge below 50% because this shortens its life (at 50% charge, the battery is producing only 12.2 volts, which may not be enough to start most marine engines). Some boaters will use a 24-volt system (two 12-volt batteries connected in parallel) to accommodate all the power requirements, while others use a 36-volt system (three 12-volt batteries).

If you have two batteries, change the selector switch to the other battery or to "both" and then try to start the engine (one battery may be designated a "starter" battery, while the other battery handles the "house load," the other electronics on board). Your boat may also have an "isolator" on board that is part of the battery-charging system. This is a diode that will keep a battery from being overcharged, which is not good for a battery's longevity. If your boat is less than 26 feet long, having a battery selector switch is not a Coast Guard requirement; if it is 26 feet or longer, the selector is required.

A battery selector switch provides positive battery disconnect, isolates all circuits, and also protects against the hazards of electrical fire and explosions. It can be separate or combined with the circuit breakers for individual circuits.

the hull, always use both negative posts—it will create an excess voltage drop, and current flow may damage the engine or other electronics on board.

64 Danger: high voltage in the water

It's a hot day and you're thinking of diving off the boat in a slip in the marina. DON'T. Most marinas have shore power hookups (AC), and for a variety of reasons, a boat may have a wire near or on an AC wire at the dock, which can put high voltage into the water. The result can be a small field of AC current as high as 120 volts, which is enough to relax your muscles to the point of drowning.

While a marine battery can be recharged with the alternator on the engine or a separate battery charger at home, it's always good to know if the battery is capable of the demand being placed on it. You may have a starting battery designated only to get the engine running when needed, and a house battery designated for handling "house loads": the bilge pump, the VHF, lights, and the refrigerator.

Here's the formula to determine the power needs of your boat:

amp draw X time used=amp hours

For example, your running lights draw 5 amps total/hour x 3 hours of use, the running lights used = 15 amp hours.

Make sure you include the amp hours of everything that is being powered by the battery(ies): GPS, stove; bilge pump-DVD player; etc.

One of the three measures of a marine battery is amp hours. Deep Cycle batteries are sold by amp hours (A-hrs), so this is one way to measure capacity. This is the amperage available when discharged evenly over a 20-hour period. But factor in all of the power draws on board as if they will be used at the same time for a specific length of time. An example of an amp-hour battery made for marine use is one with an amp-hour capacity of 73. This means it can run 1 amp for 73 hours or 73 amps for 1 hour or 36½ amps for 2 hours.

The second measure of a battery is cold cranking amperage (CCA), which is the power a battery can generate for 30 seconds at 0FF and not fall below 1.2 volts per cell. CCA ratings are used when selecting a starting battery. Know the required CCA rating for your engine and then find a battery that can accommodate the load. If you are also going to run "hotel loads" as well, a dual battery system is going to be a worthwhile choice if it hasn't been made already. Let one battery start the engine and the other run all the other stuff. Each can be recharged with an alternator that is part of your boat's electrical system.

Reserve capacity is the third measure of a marine battery. Simply put, this is the number of minutes it can maintain the necessary voltage under a 25-ampere discharge. The higher the reserve capacity of a battery, the longer it can run the electronics and lights on board. Reserve capacity is one of the features you should consider when looking for a new battery or troubleshooting problems with existing batteries.

65 Shore power cord

If you have lots of accessories on board, the shore power cord is going to become hot. The first step is to unplug it. Inspect the connectors and, if necessary, clean them. If you are handy, most connectors can be replaced at the local marine store; otherwise, get a new one. Never use a household three-prong adapter at the dock.

66 Battery storage

Place batteries in a ventilated area. Batteries can produce hydrogen gas (potentially explosive) so avoid any contact with an open flame. Secure them so they are protected from water and can't move or shift while the boat is underway. Sailboats will heel, so keep an eye out for any movement of the batteries.

Extra: THE BILGE PUMP

While bilge pumps are priced by the number of gallons they pump per hour, and while that number is usually impressive, remember the gallons per hour (gph) is based on gallons pumped horizontally. All bilge pumps are placed in the lowest part of the boat and have to pump vertically. The _actual_ pumping capacity will therefore _always be lower_ than the rated capacity.

---

67 Bilge pump not working

If you have already determined that the battery is performing as it should, the first place to check is the area beneath the bilge pump. This where the screen gets clogged with everything from hair to paper towels to whatever is floating in the bilge. Ninety percent of the time this is the cause of the problem.

Extra: MARINE BATTERIES

There are four types of marine batteries. **Never use an automobile battery on your boat.**

- Gel Cell, which is just that, is composed of chemicals in a sealed gel. They are expensive but have been shown to have a long life.

- AGM (Absorbed Glass Mat) is low maintenance and won't leak if knocked over.

- Wet Cell (also called lead acid) require inspection of fluid levels on a regular basis (use only distilled water). They are inexpensive, have a life of 2-5 years and are available as either starting batteries (to start the engine) or deep cycle batteries (to handle house loads). Wet cell batteries need to be well-ventilated during recharging.

- Dual purpose is a new design that can be used for both starting and house loads.

When buying new batteries, buy the same type, and buy them at the same time. Hooking up a new battery with an old battery is never a good idea; the ability of the new battery to recharge is affected by the old battery.

Another possible cause—and you'll see it right away—is that the pump has actually moved from its position, possibly even fallen over.

7 Electronics

According to the National Marine Manufacturers' Association, marine electronics have become the most popular product. Take a look at the cockpit of a new boat—there are screens for depth, fish, GPS, satellite radio, and chartplotters. Still, with all this information (and enter-tainment) available, the skipper should be able to have a sense of his boat's location without having to consult a screen.

68   Placement of screens

Don't let the screens obscure your view ahead, port, starboard, and aft. Arrange them so you can read all without leaving the helm. Screens are becoming larger, and there's more of a temptation to mount something in your field of vision. Don't.

69   The GPS isn't working

There are more than two dozen satellites orbiting the earth at 7,000 miles per hour at an altitude of 10,000 miles. Each crosses the equator at an angle of 55 degrees inclination and follows the same ground pattern with each pass. Using expanded triangulation (your unit on the boat is in contact with as many as 12 satellites at any given time), the GPS identifies not only your location but your speed and the direction in which you are moving. If you are wearing sunglasses and using an older model GPS without a color screen, you may not be able to see any of the data being provided.

If the GPS fails:

- Handheld units that have low battery power may flash the word "message" on the screen. This means you have less than 30 minutes of battery power remaining. Always have extra batteries. New batteries will have about 24 hours of continuous use.

- Handheld units cannot be operated in the cabin. A clear view of the sky is necessary for the signals to be received. Also check the bimini. The canvas may be too thick for the signals to penetrate through.

- Sometimes rain will settle on a handheld or deck-mounted GPS antenna. Wipe it with a dry cloth.

- If the unit hasn't been used for a while, or if it's being operated hundreds of miles from its last location, it could take up to five minutes to acquire satellite signals.

- Contact the manufacturer's technical support center and obtain "the key sequence for master reset." This can be used as a last resort when, for whatever reason, the entire unit fails. This can be done online, or through an 800 number. If done online you'll probably be able to download any applicable software upgrades.

If you are asked to give your current waypoints to friends so they can bring their boats alongside yours, here's how to do it.

- Find your waypoints on the GPS by simply turning it on (some models, like a chart plotter with GPS, always show the waypoints with a tap of the cursor on the screen). Once the GPS accesses the necessary satellites, it will show two sets of numbers and letters.

If you have waypoints for the "R1" buoy that is about a mile east of Rudee Inlet, Virginia Beach, they'll look like this on your GPS:

> 36 49.6N
> 75 57.3W

The first waypoint is always latitude. These are lines running parallel to the equator and identify your position from north to south. The numbers become higher as you move closer to the poles (the equator is 0° while the poles are 90°). If you are north of the equator, Latitude uses the letter "N"; if south of the equator, it uses the letter "S".

Longitude is the second set of waypoints and identifies the position from east to west (the numbers range from 0° at the Prime Meridian in Greenwich, England, to 180° east or west). In the United States, longitude increases as you move west, for example, while Rudee Inlet on the East Coast is 75 57.3W, the entrance to Marina del Rey Harbor near

Los Angeles is 118.46.236W. However, if you continue west, the longitude increases until it hits 180°. This is the International Dateline from which, continuing in the same direction, longitude will decrease and be identified as "E" rather than "W."

Waypoints are the intersection of latitude and longitude.

Latitude and Longitude

Latitude, left, is measured north or south from the equator (0°) to the poles (90°). Meridians of longitude and parallels of latitude are shown at 15° intervals. Longitude, right, is measured from the prime meridian (0°), which passes through Greenwich, England, east or west to a maximum of 180°.

- When giving your position, translate the symbols into words in this manner. If your chart tells you, say, that Grand Traverse Bay Lighthouse is 45°12'38N, 85°33'01W, tell the person to whom you are giving this information it is "Forty-five degrees, twelve minutes, thirty-eight seconds North, eighty-five degrees, thirty-three minutes, one second West."

- It's always a good idea to record the important waypoints you have on your GPS on a chart.

71 Depth sounder/fish finder isn't working

- The fish finder and depth sounder operate with a transducer mounted in one of three places: on the transom, underneath the hull, or inside the boat (called a "shoot through"). If it's mounted on the transom, the general rule is to place it at least 15 feet from the propeller (when the prop is turned toward it). Prop wash creates bubbles, which affect performance. If mounted inside the boat, the unit won't operate properly if there is more than one inch of single-layer fiberglass (no core or wood) thickness and unless a special attachment is used, a shoot through won't be able to monitor speed or water temperature.

- If the boat is on a trailer, see if a bunk or roller has dislodged or damaged the transducer during launching or retrieval. If it has, you'll need to find another location. Transducers should be mounted parallel to the water bottom.

Extra: DEPTH-SOUNDER ALARMS

Most depth sounders have depth alarms, which will start beeping/making noise when the boat's bottom is within a predetermined distance from the water's bottom. If you are traveling at a high rate of speed, there may not be enough time to slow down the boat or change course before you find yourself in shallow water. Depth is measured using "low mean water"—this is the average depth at low tide. But strong winds and certain tides can make "low mean water" even lower.

- If you have this problem in shallow water (less than 15 feet), turn the sensitivity down on the unit. Or turn the instrument to "manual range" and set for 5 to 10 feet.

- The transducer requires cleaning from time to time, especially if the boat is kept in the water. Use detergent.

- Sometimes other instruments on the boat will cause an electrical interference, usually identified by a constant beeping. With the boat at the dock and everything off but the unit, begin turning on every piece of equipment individually. When the problem starts, the last piece of equipment turned on is the culprit. Run the engine and trolling motor as well to see if they could be the cause. The next step is to inspect the grounding system.

- If you have installed a livewell pickup (this is a pipe that brings fresh water into the livewell on the boat to keep fish alive) in line and in front of the transducer, this too will disturb the accuracy of the reading it provides.

Extra: IF YOUR DEPTH FINDER-FAILS

If your depth finder fails, carry a handheld lead line. This is a length of line (10 to 20 feet) with a weight on one end. It is marked off in one-foot measurements, usually by placing a piece of tape every 12 inches, and it can be quickly dropped over the side to determine the depth of the water. Some folks even mark their boat's draft on the line.

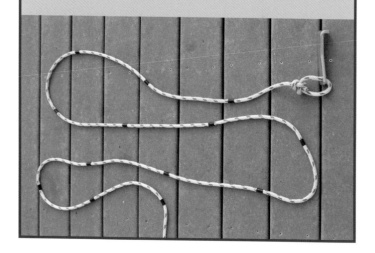

The speedometer on your boat shows a speed different from that shown on the GPS.

The speedometer on your boat measures the speed over water and is calculated with a paddlewheel or intake tubes that measure water pressure (the faster you go, the higher the pressure). But the boat is also affected by wind and currents. GPS measures the boat's speed over ground, which is simply the distance between point A and point B without factoring in wind and currents. Algae or weeds can get into the speedometer paddlewheel and the intake tubes can become clogged (clean with a pin) so this can affect the result you are seeing. Though not common, the paddlewheel may have lost one or two of its spokes from the hull hitting debris while underway. Sometimes, and this, too, is rare, it can lose magnetism as a result of electrical current in the water (most often in a marina).

Extra: IF YOUR SPEEDOMETER FAILS

If your speedometer fails and the need to know your speed is essential, gather a long line and put a knot in it every 23.2 feet. Drop it off the stern and count the number of "knots" that run out in 15 seconds. That's your boat's speed, and that's why a boat's speed is measured in "knots."

73 Chartplotter troubles

Chartplotters are the new "must-haves" in boating. They are electronic versions of the charts you have on board and are combined with a GPS receiver in a computer screen showing your boat's position relative to buoys, marinas, and other waypoints.

- If the chartplotter won't turn on, unplug every other electronic device on board and see if the instrument will operate on its own. If so, the chartplotter is being shorted by one of the other instruments. Now you will have to turn the chartplotter on and individually plug in the other instruments to find the source of the problem.

- If you are using a multifunction screen with radar, disconnect the radar from the unit.

- You may be able to correct the problem by letting the engine(s) run for about five minutes; this can provide the needed charge for a battery that may have run down.

A common complaint: "Every time I want to call a friend on his boat, the VHF channels are filled with chatter." Before leaving the dock agree with the friends you want to contact on a time and a channel to do so; e.g., twenty after the hour on channel 68, and if that's crowded, agree on an alternate channel. Then synchronize your watches to make sure the plan works.

- Avoid asking for a radio check on channel 16. Go instead to one of the boater-to-boater channels to make the request. This helps alleviate heavy use of an already crowded radio channel.

- If another boater is talking, wait until that conversation concludes before talking. If you are using a 3-watt VHF radio, it may be overwhelmed by others using a 5- or 6-watt VHF.

- If the boater or marina you are contacting is nearby, use low power.

Channels Used by Recreational Boaters

It is important to understand that although your VHF radio has many channels, each is designated for a specific use.

Channels 16 and 9 are used for initial contact with another boater (briefly) or to contact the Coast Guard in the event of a serious problem (sinking, illness, boat collision, accident). Always monitor channel 16. Distress signals begin here.

Channel 1, 2, 3 are designated for NOAA Marine Forecast (receive only).

Channel 9 is used for hailing other boats (this channel exists to relieve the congestion on channel 16). Some lock and bridge tenders use channel 9 to contact boaters.

Channel 13 is used for contact between boaters and lock/bridge tenders and for contact between commercial vessels (including tugs) and vessels more than 65.6 feet in length.

Channels 68, 69, 71, 72 and 72A are working channels used by recreational boaters (non-commercial) for ship-to-ship and ship-to-shore (harbors and marinas) communication.

Extra: VHF—WHAT YOU NEED TO KNOW

VHF (very high frequency) operates best with line of sight, although many fixed-mount VHFs operate with antennas mounted on the mast or fly bridge, which allows contact with boats as far as 25 miles away.

- How far will your VHF reach? Use this formula: square root of height above water X 1.42 = transmit range in miles.

- Newer VHF radios are equipped with digital selective calling (DSC). In the event of an emergency, all DSC radios have a red distress button. Once pressed, your radio is connected to the Coast Guard. You should provide the names of the boat and its owner; your location in longitude and latitude and any identifying landmarks. Switch to channel 16, where you will be able to speak to a duty officer about your problem.

  Other boats with DSC will be alerted and may be able to assist if the situation warrants it. The Coast Guard is now aware of your situation and location and can easily send assistance.

- These radios must be connected to an on-board GPS and registered with the Coast Guard. You will receive a maritime mobile service identity (MMSI) number at www.boatus.com/mmsi/.

Extra: WHAT'S THAT HUM?

If a power cable is run through the boat next to an aerial wire (a wire that is attached to a VHF radio or even an AM/FM/SW radio), the result is radio frequency interference (RFI), which may manifest itself as a constant hum in the reception. Move the power wire away from the aerial wire. Grounding the instrument may reduce the RFI but it won't eliminate it.

8 Maintaining Your Boat

As the skipper of a vessel, you'll be expected not only to make informed, often quick, decisions while your boat is underway but also to bring the same sense of importance and preparation to the care and maintenance of your boat while it is sitting at the dock or on a trailer going nowhere.

75 Aquatic nuisance species (ANS)

Zebra mussels, round gobies, and sea lampreys are among the many aquatic nuisance species found in lakes and rivers throughout the United States.

It is believed that an international tanker emptied thousands of gallons of water from its ballast tanks in Lake St. Clair in 1988, releasing zebra mussels that had been carried across the Atlantic Ocean. Because they have no known predator, zebra mussels have multiplied rapidly throughout inland freshwater lakes, clogging city and power plant water-intake pipes.

The only benefit of zebra-mussel infestation in the Great Lakes is that they filter the water and have made it cleaner. But these and other aquatic nuisance species have slowly spread to the west, hitching rides on boats and boat trailers. Today, many marinas and boat ramps are posting signs warning of the presence of ANS and asking all boats and trailers be inspected prior to launch and after retrieval for any ANS that may be aboard. It is important that you wash your hull and trailer after the boat has been retrieved from one body of water and before it is launched into another body of water. The water from a baitwell should be returned to the source—never empty it into another lake. If there's mud on your anchor, clean it off before using the anchor in another body of water. For more information about what to do and what not to do regarding ANS, visit www.anstaskforce.gov.

76   Wet-cell battery

Fill your wet-cell battery (also called "lead acid" battery) with distilled water only.

77   Need to measure?

- No ruler or tape measure on board? Maybe this'll help: A dollar bill measures 6⅛ inches long by 2⅝ inches wide.

- Use a crescent or pipe wrench to measure the diameter of a pipe/hose that is still attached and needs replacing. Put the wrench around the hose and measure the width. That's the outside diameter. Most hoses/pipes are measured by outside diameter.

78   The fender board

To make docking easier, build a fender board with two or three of your fenders. It's simply a three- to four-foot piece of 2x4 with holes drilled where the fenders will be located. Tie the fenders on the board and hang it over the side of the hull with the fenders against the hull and the board against the pilings.

- **Outboard Engines:** Start the engine and disconnect the fuel line. This removes all unused fuel in the line (and engine). If the outboard is too heavy to be taken off the boat and stored, fill the fuel tank and add stabilizer. Leave the vent open so gases can't expand during periods of warm temperature. Change the oil (old oil may contain corrosive compounds) and lower-unit fluid. If keeping the boat in the water leave the engine down (it will keep the lower unit from freezing).

- **I/O Engines:** If an I/O is being stored in the water, leave the outdrive down; run antifreeze into the engine.

- **If your boat is stored on land:** Remove batteries and recharge them every 30 to 60 days when not in use. Run antifreeze into the engine. Fog the carburetor while the engine is running. No boat should ever be placed on jackstands if the ground is soft, wet, or subject to flooding. If the ground is gravel, use plywood under the jackstand.

- **If any boat is stored in the water:** Make a routine inspection, especially after a big snowfall. The weight of melting snow can be sufficient to sink a boat with clogged or frozen drains.

- **If you have a propane stove (LPG):** Disconnect the tank from the supply line and install a protective plug in the tank.

- **Trailer boats:** Remove the drain plug and raise the bow (a piece of wood under the trailer-tongue jack will work) so that water can drain out the plughole.

- Take any valuable electronic equipment off the boat. Remove any foodstuffs as well.

- If you are parking your trailer outside, place it on a concrete surface, not grass. Moisture from grass or bare ground can damage trailer tires and possibly corrode the frame. If the trailer is parked in your driveway, face the tongue away from the street; this makes it more difficult to steal.

- Take high winds and nearby trees into account when assessing potential causes of damage to your boat.

80 Spring startup

A checklist of things to do, places on your boat to inspect, and equipment to test and/or replace to make your vessel seaworthy for the upcoming season on the water:

- Inspect and lubricate seacocks.

- Inspect hoses and hose clamps and replace as necessary.

- Replace deteriorated anodes on outdrive, outboard, trim tabs.

- Inspect prop(s) for dings, pitting, and distortion. Make sure the cotter pins are secure. Grip the prop and try moving the shaft. If it's loose, the cutlass bearing may need to be replaced.

- Make sure your engine intake sea strainer is free of corrosion and properly secured.

- Check the engine shaft and rudder stuffing boxes for looseness. After the boat is launched, be sure to check them again as well as through-hulls for leaks.

- Use a hose to spray the boat's ports and hatches to check for deck leaks. Renew caulking or gaskets as necessary.

- Inspect rubber outdrive bellows for cracked, dried, and/or deteriorated spots (look especially in the folds) and replace if suspect.

- Check power-steering and power-trim oil levels.

- Inspect outer jacket of control cables. Cracks or swelling indicate corrosion and the cable has to be replaced.

- Inspect fuel lines, including fill and vent hoses, for softness, brittleness, or cracking. Check all joints for leaks and make sure all lines are well supported with smooth-edged noncombustible clips or straps.

- Inspect fuel tanks, fuel pumps, and filters for leaks. Clamps should be snug and free of rust. Clean fuel filters.

- Inspect cooling hoses and fittings for stiffness, rot, leaks, and/or cracking. Make sure they fit snugly and are double clamped.

- Every few years, remove and inspect exhaust manifold for corrosion.

- Clean and tighten electrical connections, especially both ends of battery cables. Wire-brush battery terminals and fill cells with distilled water.

- Inspect bilge blower hose for leaks.

- Inspect all fittings for cracks and rust. Inspect wire halyards and running backstays for fishhooks (wire that is beginning to unravel) and rust.

- Check expiration dates on flares and fire extinguishers.

- Check the stove and remove tanks with loose fittings and leaking hoses.

- Inspect bilge pump and float switch to make sure they're working properly.

- Inspect dock and anchor lines for chafing.

- Update or replace old charts and waterway guides.

- Check shore power cable connections for burns, which indicate that the cable needs to be replaced.

- Make sure that your boating license and registration are up to date. Don't forget your trailer tags.

- Review your boat insurance policy and update coverage if need be. Be sure you have fuel-spill insurance coverage.

- Recycle shrink-wrap that was used during the winter. If your boat is less than 26 feet, www.dr-shrink.com will provide a package that can be returned with the used shrink-up and recycled.

Extra: WATERLINE STAINS

A hull left in the water for a period of time is going to develop waterline stains as a result of decomposing leaves that have stained the water (with tannin) among other causes. There are a number of products available in marine supply stores that will remove the stain. They all contain oxylic acid, but try simple lemon juice on the surface first. When using any product with oxylic acid, the preferred method of application is when the boat is out of the water.

Trailer Boats

- Inspect tire threads and sidewalls for cracks or lack of tread and replace as necessary. Check the air pressure in the tires, and don't forget the spare!

- Inspect bearings and replace as necessary.

- Test tail and backup lights. Test the winch to make sure it's working properly.

- Inspect trailer frame for rust. Sand and paint to prevent further deterioration.

- Secure the drain plug.

81   Bugs?

Make a cookie out of flour, sugar, and boric acid. It's not poisonous to you, but for cockroaches it's the last meal.

82   Keeping algae and barnacles off the hull

- Bottom paint or antifouling paint will improve your boat's performance on the water because it will keep algae and barnacles off the hull—for a while. From time to time, take the boat to shallow water, get in with a brush (and helpers with brushes), and scrub the hull below the waterline. Some marinas offer a brief powerwash for just such a purpose.

- Before you go shopping for new bottom or antifouling paint, know what you have on your boat. Not all paints are compatible with one another.

83   Through hulls

Every through-hull fitting should have a seacock to shut off water entry should a hose fail, or to work on equipment served by that fitting. A solid pipe extending to above the waterline, not shown here, is a desirable added safety feature.

A survey of causes of outboard-powered boats sinking at the dock conducted by BoatU.S. Marine Insurance concludes that the second most common reason is the failure of underwater (below the waterline) through-hull fittings. (The first is heavy rain, which causes drains to clog; the weight of the extra, undrained water, at 8.3 pounds to the gallon, sinks the boat.)

Know the number and location of all through hulls on your boat. Located below the waterline, a safe through-hull fitting is made of either bronze or Marelon. If your boat has plastic hulls, this is the time to consider replacing them. If you aren't sure, take a knife and scrape the edge of the through hull. If it's bronze, you'll know right away, but be advised: if the color is red or pink, this is an indication the bronze fitting is deteriorating. Marelon is made by RC Marine and is a special fiberglass/nylon material.

Through hulls operate with a hand lever that opens or closes a ball valve (older boats may have a gate valve, and that's another good reason to replace them), allowing water into an engine intake or a head intake or for any number of purposes. Move the handle into the desired position a few times to

ensure it operates with ease. In some cases it may be necessary to lubricate the handle with a few drops of WD-40. Inspect through hulls a few times every year. This is one area of maintenance that, if neglected, can ruin your day's outing—or, possibly, your boat.

If you operate in saltwater, wash the boat down with freshwater after every trip. If you trailer your boat, wash both because if left on the hull and trailer frame and allowed to dry in the sun or the wind, saltwater will leave a coating that not only dulls the finish but makes future cleaning all the more labor intensive. If you boat in freshwater, a thorough rinse of boat and trailer is just as important.

Extra: GREEN CLEANING

- Use only products that are biodegradable, phosphate free, and nontoxic. Don't use detergents that contain bleach or ammonia. Visit a marine-supply store rather than a supermarket for boat-cleaning products.

- Equal amounts of baking soda and vinegar used on a sponge can "green clean" a hull.

- Air freshener. Leave an open box of baking soda exposed to the air.

- Cleaning brass. Mix Worcestershire sauce or a paste of equal parts of salt and vinegar with water.

- Don't empty the contents of your cleaning bucket in the water. Dispose of this waste on land.

85　Lines

Your dock lines may chafe after a while as a result of rubbing against metal chocks on the boat. A simple way to protect them is to cut a piece of used garden hose that is long enough to protect the line where it comes in contact with the metal chock and then slice it lengthwise, putting the hose around the line where it passes through the chock. You can tape the ends of the hose around the line to keep it from sliding.

9 Messes and Emergencies

A skipper is judged a "good" skipper not by the way they behave when things are going well, but how they react in moments of emergency. At sea, quick decisions are required. One's options are limited, and time is of the essence.

86 Man overboard!

Make this important topic a part of your dockside, pre-trip briefing of the crew. Instruct them that should a passenger go over the side, someone must remain on deck to point out his/her position. If you are the only person on deck, don't go below—for any reason. Keep your eyes on the person in the water, and do the following—immediately.

- Yell, "Man overboard!" and toss a life preserver, a cushion, or a ring buoy; in fact, toss several cushions as a way to make a "trail." If the person in the water can swim, the  cushion or ring buoy can be used as a signal to other boaters, who may not be able to see him/her.

- If you have a handheld GPS, immediately hit the "mark," or MOB, button so your location is recorded. Look at your compass heading. When you make the turn, set a course 180 degrees from the direction in which you were going.

- Slow down and turn toward the person in the water; make your approach going against the wind and the waves so as to avoid being pushed into, and possibly injuring, the person you're trying to help.

- Take note of the boat traffic, and if any nearby boat presents a threat to the person in the water, contact the skipper on Channel 16 and/or wave him off.

- When you are close to the person in the water, put the engine in neutral. If there is a crewmember available, have him/her drop the anchor.

- If necessary, send a crewmember into the water with a life jacket that has a line attached to the boat. In this way, the victim can be pulled in.

- Have a plan as to how a person overboard can be safely returned to the boat, whether by way of the swim ladder, swim platform, or halyard from the mast and a winch. If you have an outboard or an I/O engine that can be raised and lowered, the person in the water may be able to lie across the outdrive and be pulled aboard—with the assistance of others—as the engine comes up.

- When assisting the rescued person into the boat, don't pull on the life jacket. It could come off.

Hypothermia

Humans lose body heat 25 times faster in the water than they do in the air. If the body temperature has dropped 2-3°, hypothermia has begun.

- If you are in the water, and are wearing a life jacket, think of the word "HELP"—and use a Heat Escape Lessening Position by pulling your legs up while clasping your arms around your chest. If you have no life jacket, the HELP position can't be used because you'll have to tread water. Move as little as possible because heat will escape from your body with every motion made.

- Position yourself with the waves at your back. By doing so, your mouth and nose are kept clear of spray.

- Once aboard, the person's wet clothing should be removed and they need to be wrapped in blankets (towels, sleeping bags) and, if possible, moved out of the wind.

- Don't massage their arms or legs because this can result in heat loss.

- Despite what is done in the movies, no alcoholic beverages. A hot drink (tea or coffee) will help increase the body temperature.

Seasickness

A person suffering from seasickness will become quiet. That's the first sign that something isn't right. Seasickness occurs when the inner ear, which maintains equilibrium in humans when they are on land, can no longer do its job because of the motion of the boat on the water. Here's what to do:

- Don't let a person suffering from seasickness go below, despite his/her protests to do so.

- Keep him/her focused on the horizon.

- If nausea hasn't kicked in, give the person a chance to handle the helm. This way he/she can stay busy and concentrate on something besides how miserable he/she may feel.

- Pills: Dramamine and other antinausea medications work, but they have to be taken several hours before heading out to sea. Some boaters report getting good results from using wristbands which exert pressure on the underside of the wrist (the median nerve at P6—the Neiguan acupuncture point) but must be worn for a while before getting on the boat.

Diabetes

Sun, wind, and the motion of the boat, as well as being active (swimming, waterskiing, tubing), can lower a person's blood sugar to the point where he/she becomes drowsy, argumentative, nauseous, and may even appear inebriated. If the diabetic carries glucose tablets (and many do), urge him/her to take as many as four. If no tablets are available, a glass of fruit juice or a soda (not diet, not sugar-free) will quickly raise the blood-sugar level. Normal range is considered to be 100 to 120. Diabetics often carry glucose meters with them.

Heart Attack

Symptoms include chest discomfort, shortness of breath and a feeling of nausea. Treatment is essential and must be given within one hour of the first symptom. This is called "the golden hour."

- Call 911 (or press "CG" on the keypad). If you aren't within a working cell, use the VHF and contact the Coast Guard on Channel 16. Be ready to provide your boat description and location (waypoints).

- Have the person take an aspirin. This thins the blood.

Heat Stroke

The medical definition is the body temperature has reached 103°. Symptoms are a lack of sweating, pale skin, disorientation and an accelerated heart rate.

- Move the person out of direct sunlight. Have them lie down and elevate their feet.

- Place ice wrapped in a towel on the patient's head, back of their neck, in the palms of their hands or the back of their wrists. If possible, sponge some cool water on these areas too. Have them drink cold water.

Sunburn

It can be difficult to know when your skin has burned when the boat is going at high speeds. But when you or your "crew" realize what has happened, it's too late for any kind of prevention. First, get out of the sun and no matter how hot it may be, wear a long sleeve shirt or put a towel over your shoulder and wear a baseball cap or any kind of hat. Aloe vera has proven to be effective in providing relief. If blisters are visible, this indicates a second degree burn and a trip to the hospital may be necessary.

88 Noxious odors

If the odor is coming from the water tank, drain the tank and refill it adding a half cup of bleach. Then drain the tank again and refill. Also, check the water hoses (water hoses are always white) and consider replacing them. An old hose with decaying matter clinging to the inside wall can add odor to the water passing through it.

89 Birds

If you have a boat in the water, you are well aware what seagulls, cormorants, herons, and everything else that can fly will do if given the chance. And they are given the chance.

Marine-supply stores sell replicas of owls that are meant to hang—scarecrow-like—from a stanchion or bimini frame to ward off unwelcome avian visitors. And they will work, providing their locations are changed frequently, as in every other day. If you leave the owls in one place the seagulls will catch on to the ruse.

Other boaters have reported success using colored flags—the kind you see at used-car lots. Run them from the bow to the cockpit and to the stern so they can flap in the breeze and scare off the birds, and prevent them from "dropping" in. There are a variety of cleaning agents available if the scarecrow/flag strategies don't work.

90 Fire

The story is told—it may be apocryphal but it certainly is common—of a couple preparing dinner on their anchored boat in the Florida Keys. Their charcoal grill was attached to the stern pulpit. The wind was moderate and the boat was pointed into it, and the smoke from the grill was blowing off the stern just as it should. But the couple had a dinghy tied to the stern, and a spark from the grill landed on the gas tank for the dinghy's outboard motor. Dinner had to wait until the fire was extinguished.

The lesson? Tie the dinghy (and its gasoline engine and fuel tank) out of the line of sparks and fire.

- Fire extinguishers—Boats use not only charcoal as a fuel source for cooking but kerosene, liquid petroleum gas (LPG, also called "propane") and alcohol as well. (LPG is becoming more common; refills are widely available and easy to attach.) Regardless of the kind of fuel you're using, make sure there's a fire extinguisher within easy reach.

  Fire extinguishers are identified by their ability to put out a specific kind of fire. The Tri-Class extinguisher (get several of them) is effective in putting out all three classes of fire: (A) wood, fiberglass, cloth; (B) gasoline, diesel fuel, cooking-stove fuel; (C) electrical. It is a dry-chemical extinguisher, recommended for use on boats less than 65 feet by the American Boat and Yacht Council (ABYC) and approved by the U.S. Coast Guard.

- If possible, head the boat so that the fire is blowing away from rather than into the boat.

- Engine fires are first detected by the sight or smell of smoke coming from the engine vents or a sudden change in rpms. The natural reaction is to open the engine compartment to see what's going on. Don't. This will only allow air to fuel the fire. Many engines—yours should be among them—have fire ports to which a gaseous fire extinguisher, which takes oxygen out of the fire, can be attached.

91   Leaking hose

Your engine has hoses, your through-hull fittings are connected to hoses, and when one of them fails, you may not even notice. Suffice it to say, eventually you will notice—and it won't be pretty. That's why it's always worth your time to do frequent inspections of the hoses. To state the obvious: A leaking hose, whether it's carrying water or fuel, is dangerous.

- A quick, albeit temporary, fix to a leaking hose can be accomplished by placing a larger diameter section of hose over the leak and securing it on both ends with hose clamps.

Extra: RAIN AND SNOW

Your boat has cockpit drains (also called "scuppers"), which allow water from waves as well as rain to flow out of the cockpit and back into the water. Should these drains become clogged with leaves or twigs, the water will remain inside the cockpit. As the water level increases (remember: water weighs 8.3 pounds to the gallon), the boat is going to sit lower in the water. If the boat remains at a marina throughout a winter during which there was a heavy fall of snow, the snow may melt while the drains are still clogged with ice. Boats have been known to sink at the dock for this reason. So, after the rains come or the snow falls, you always have a good reason to visit your boat.

Most of the time things go smoothly at the fuel dock, but when they don't, a real mess is at hand. So consider these time-tested pointers when thinking about filling up or topping off.

- Before approaching the fuel dock, pick a spot you know will be able to handle your boat's length. Remember, you are going to have to approach at an angle, which means you'll need more available length than just that of your boat. Some fuel docks employ dockhands and have lines available, which certainly make a landing easier.

- Decide which side of the boat will be against the dock. It's always preferable to have the side with the fuel-fill opening (the fuel cap) closest to the dock within easy reach of the fuel hose. Have fenders dropped on that side, and position two crewmembers, each with a line, one at the bow and one at the stern. In general a 30-degree approach should be made to the dock either bowfirst or sternfirst (depending on wind and current conditions).

- Make certain everyone on board knows the drill.

- An often-used technique is coming in bow first at an angle and a crewmember with a bow line in hand gets off the boat (without pushing too hard and pushing the bow out).

The stern line is then tossed and the crewmember has both lines and pulls the boat into the dock.

- Know the capacity of your tank and the amount of fuel you're going to need.

- Before refueling, shut off the engine, turn off all electrical appliances and heat sources and close cabin doors, portals, and hatches.

- Everyone should disembark during refueling, but stress that this will be a brief stop and that they should stay close by so as not to delay others waiting to refuel.

- Concentrate. Make sure it's the fuel fill you're opening and not the water or waste fill.

- While filling (note: fuel at a marina comes out faster than fuel at a gas station), monitor closely for any spillage, and have a rag in your hand to clean up any spills.

- Once the tank is filled, operate the blower for five minutes before starting the engine. Open hatches and companionways.

- It is considered good etiquette to tip dockhands who have assisted you with the lines.

Emergency and the VHF

There are three levels of priority for emergency VHF radio calls. When you hear one, get off the channel and allow the transmission to be completed and answered.

93 Mayday (from the French, "m'aider" = help me)

This is the most serious scenario. If your boat is sinking or if someone on board is seriously injured or ill, key in channel 16 and say:

"Mayday, Mayday, Mayday. This is the (vessel's name)." [Repeat the boat's name three times.]

"Mayday. The vessel (name) is located (state your position; waypoints are best, or a geographical reference, e.g., one mile north of channel marker number . . .)."

Now state the nature of the emergency and the number of people on board. Sign off by repeating the name of the boat one more time. Unkey the transmit button.

The Coast Guard may respond with a request for a long count (one . . . two . . . three . . . four . . .) to give them time for their direction finders to fix on your location.

94   Pan-pan (pronounced "pawn-pawn")

The second most serious scenario, where life may not be at stake — yet — but conditions are such that they could get worse (fighting fire on board but no injuries; taking on water, but so far everything is under control). This is not a call for help as much as it is an attempt to alert potential rescuers of your situation and location. Key in channel 16 and say:

"Pawn-pawn, pawn-pawn, pawn-pawn. This is the (vessel's name)." [Repeat the boat's name three times.]

Now indicate your location (waypoints, landmarks), followed by a description of your situation.

End transmission with a final repetition of your boat's name and unkey channel 16.

95   Securité (pronounced "Securi-tay")

If you see a potential navigation hazard — a piling floating in a channel; a channel marker without red or green designation or number; your boat is disabled in an inlet during a heavy fog — key in channel 16 and say:

"Securité, securité, securité. This is the (vessel's name)." [Repeat the boat's name three times.]

Now describe the nature and location of the navigation hazard.

End transmission with a final repetition of the boat's name and unkey channel 16.

10

Bad Weather

Despite the weather forecast, the marine weather radio announcements, and your own careful preparation, sometimes you'll find yourself facing a storm on the water. But weather always provides clues as to what is to come.

96 The barometer

A rising barometer is a sign of good weather; a falling barometer tells you bad weather is on the way. This is the instrument that tells us whether a high-pressure system (good weather) or a low-pressure system (bad weather) is approaching.

- If the barometer falls rapidly, expect strong winds; if the rate of change over an hour is 0.02, there's no need for alarm, though you should be seeking shelter or heading back to the dock. If the rate of change is 0.05, this is cause for concern.

- If the wind is blowing from the south to the southeast while the barometer falls, a storm is approaching from the west or northwest, and its center will pass near or north of your position within 12 to 24 hours with the wind veering to the northwest from the south and then from the southwest.

- If the wind is coming from the east and northeast while the barometer falls rapidly, the storm is approaching from the south or southwest, and its center will be south of your position with the wind backing to the northwest by way of north.

97 Storm approaching

Which way? If you see threatening clouds in the distance and want to get an idea of the direction in which they are traveling, use the Buys-Ballot's Law. This is a simple way to determine if you are in the path of the approaching weather. With your back to the wind and your arms extended, low pressure (bad weather) is to the left and high pressure (better weather) is to the right. This simple law has allowed many boaters to get out of harm's way and find calmer waters.

98 Clouds

There are three kinds of clouds:

- Cirrus are high, thin clouds (18,000 to 20,000 feet) caused by warm air being lifted by an approaching cold front within the next 24 hours. They may have a fibrous (hairlike) appearance or a silky sheen, or both.

Cirrus

- Cumulus are middle altitude clouds (7,000 to 18,000 feet) known for their puffy cotton-ball shape. Cumulus clouds portend fair weather, although they can develop into cumulonimbus clouds associated with late-afternoon thunderstorms (the prefix/suffix "nimbo" means "rain"). Squall winds can reach 50 knots in gusts with accompanying torrential rain.

Cumulus

Cumulonimbus

- Stratus are low-level clouds (ground level to 7,000 feet) and occur because warm air is rising above cooler air. They have a thick, almost uniform look, indicating stable air. As there is little turbulence here, any precipitation would be in the form of a fine drizzle. Nimbostratus clouds can block out the sun during bad weather.

Stratus

Nimbostratus

Cumulonimbus clouds carry a positive charge, whereas the ground has a negative charge. When the buildup of opposite charges becomes great enough, the air between the clouds and the ground isn't able to insulate the path between the positive and negative charges. That's when lightning strikes, carrying as much as 100 million volts.

- Once you see the anvil shape of the cumulonimbus cloud, know that lightning is possible—anytime.

- Lower antennas and outriggers and drop anchor if you intend to ride out the bad weather in a sheltered area (avoid water that is too shallow). As the storm comes through, lightning will strike the highest objects, e.g., sailboat masts, VHF antennas.

> **Lightning from the west or northwest will reach you; lightning from the south or southeast will pass you by.**
>
> This advice applies to the northern latitudes. Lightning and storm clouds come from the west and move east. If storm activity is seen to the south, you aren't in its path.

- Go below. Don't touch metallic objects, e.g., throttles, searchlights, electronic equipment.

- Disconnect power cables from expensive equipment, e.g., chartplotters, GPS, stereo/DVD players, laptops.

- Observe the 30-30 Rule: If the time elapsed between seeing a lightning flash and hearing thunder exceeds 30 seconds, the thunderstorm is about 6 miles away. When the time elapsed becomes less than 30 seconds, your boat is vulnerable to a lightning strike. You should wait 30 minutes after the storm passes before leaving the anchorage, because lightning strikes are still possible. Thunderstorms move at about 20 miles per hour.

Once a storm becomes a hurricane (winds in excess of
74 mph), the National Hurricane Center begins to track
possible landfall areas. A "hurricane watch" is issued
36 hours before estimated landfall; a "hurricane warning"
is issued 24 hours before estimated landfall, so before hurricane season (June 1 to November 30) begins, you'll need to
have a plan that considers the following issues:

- Where the boat will stay. Studies show that boats kept
  ashore fare better in a hurricane than boats left in the
  water. Many marinas have organized "hurricane clubs,"
  which, for a fee, will pull your boat out of the water and
  move it to higher ground before the hurricane hits. (Some
  insurance companies will cover the cost of this benefit.)

- If your boat is on a trailer, you have options: You can
  move it to a location out of the storm's path, find a secure
  storage facility that is built to withstand hurricane-force
  winds, or secure it in your backyard. If you choose the
  latter, remove as much equipment as possible, fill the hull
  with water (the increased weight will make it more difficult for the boat to be moved by high winds), be aware of
  nearby hazards that could fall on or be blown into your
  boat, e.g., trees, telephone poles and wires, lawn furniture,
  playground equipment, barbecue utensils.

Extra: FARADAY'S CAGE

Many ABYC lightning protection systems are based on a simple principle propounded by Michael Faraday in 1836: A lightning strike can be carried to the ground (water) if all metal conductors between the strike and the ground are bonded together. Usually a boat will have an external ground plate on the outside of the hull below the waterline where the charge is dissipated into the water. Metal on board is connected with No. 4-gauge wire through which the charge is carried. This doesn't protect against a lightning strike; in fact, it might increase the chances of one, but Faraday's Cage can provide an access for the charge into the water rather than through the hull of the boat.

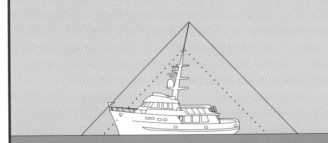

- Boat lift. This can be a tough choice. In a torrential rain, the hull could fill with water and the added weight could collapse the lift. A storm surge could raise the boat off the lift or even take the lift itself off the piling. Take it off the lift.

- 3 Things to Know about Hurricane Holes

  1. If you chose to move your boat to a sheltered location and must go under drawbridges, municipalities and state officials will close drawbridges after a certain period of time to accommodate evacuations.
  2. In a hurricane hole, boats are secured with a combination of anchors and lines tied ashore.
  3. Keep the bow facing toward the entrance of the hole because the surge will come in from that direction.

- Don't even think about staying on board during a hurricane.

If you are heading out and see any of these flags on a Coast Guard Station, turn around and reschedule your outing for another day.

- Small-craft advisory: While there is no specific definition for what constitutes a "small craft," this warning is a general alert that weather conditions may be hazardous to small vessels. The conditions necessary to issue such an alert can vary by location; for example, an advisory is posted in Georgia and Texas when winds exceed 20 knots, while in Maine, South Carolina, Lake Erie, and Lake Ontario the same advisory is posted only when winds exceed 25 knots. Acquaint yourself with local regulations.

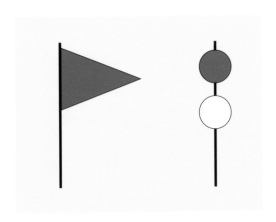

- A gale warning is issued when winds reach 34 to 47 knots.

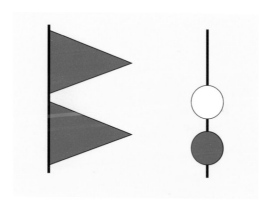

- A storm warning is issued when winds exceed 48 knots.

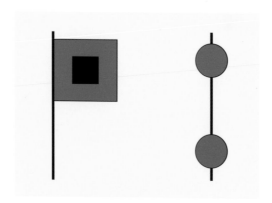

- A hurricane warning is issued when winds are in excess of 64 knots. One should monitor local radio and television broadcasts for announcements of watches and warnings.

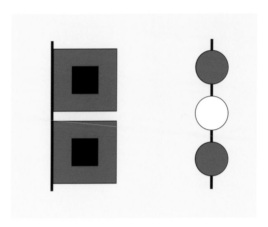

Weather reports have always been a part of civilization. Today, despite all the modern gadgets available to every boater, these weather proverbs continue to be valid. Use them, with caution, and adapt them to local waters.

A backing wind says storms are nigh, but a veering wind will clear the sky.
A wind that veers changes its direction to your right as you face it and indicates fair weather. A backing wind changes direction to your left as you face it and come from a low-pressure area.

When a halo rings the moon or sun, the rain will come upon the run.
According to the national Weather Service, halos around the sun have been followed by rain 75% of the time. Halos around the moon forecast rain 65% of the time. A halo is created by the refraction of light off ice crystals in cirrus clouds.

Rainbow to windward, foul fall the day.
Rainbow to leeward, rain runs away.
If a rainbow lies in the direction of the prevailing wind, the moisture in the air is moving toward you; however, if the rainbow is leeward, the rain has already passed.

Extra: IN A FOG

The best way to deal with fog is to do everything possible to avoid it. If there's fog at the marina, wait it out. As the sun heats the air, fog is usually "burned off" as the ground warms. The air on top of the cloud (fog) is heated first, so fog will "burn off" from top to bottom. Your boat may have all kinds of electronic mapping gear but fog has a long history of causing collisions—with other boats, with rocks, and with land. Don't think you can outsmart fog. Stay out of it.

But sometimes you just can't avoid it. Fog does occur while on the water. You may even see the fog bank rolling in. This is the moment to let everyone on board know what is taking place and what needs to be done. It's bad enough that you can't see in fog, but fog can make a minor mistake become a major mishap.

- Most important: identify your position. Do this by knowing where your boat is in relation to the shoreline and its location on a chart. Read your GPS and hit the "go-to" button with the waypoints for your marina or boat ramp. If you rely solely on the GPS because land-marks can't be seen, remember that GPS operates in straight lines and doesn't factor in sandbars, peninsulas, shipping channels, or any other potentially dangerous obstruction on the water. If possible, follow the route on your GPS back to your starting point. If you have a chart-plotter onboard, you can follow the map.

- Consider just staying where you are and dropping anchor—if there is no boat traffic and you are a distance from a channel. The fog will lift.

- If you are underway and become enveloped in a fog bank, follow these four procedures:

1. Turn off any music, DVD, radio. etc. You may not be able to see but you can hear, and this is the moment to become attuned to your surroundings. The only radio in use should be Channel 16 on the VHF. From time to time, slow the boat down and turn off the engine to hear the horns from other boats.

2. Post a lookout on the bow to warn of hazards ahead or of surf sounds that could indicate breaking waves near a shore-line and shallow water.

3. Go slow.

4. You are required to use a horn in fog whether underway or not.

   - One Long Blast (four seconds) every two minutes while underway.

   - Two long blasts followed by two short blasts every two minutes when not underway, as when anchored or fishing.

   - Two long blasts each with an interval of two seconds every two minutes when drifting.

Index

Photo credits